THE REAL LIFE XP GROWTH ENGINE

BY ALVIN C. HILL IV, MBA
aka Coach JP

THE POWER OF THE REAL LIFE XP GROWTH ENGINE

I didn't create the Real Life XP Growth Engine from theory. I built it from the trenches. Before Real Life Business Solutions ever crossed six figures, before the coaching calls, the systems, the courses, the software, and the marketing engine there was just me. A man trying to rebuild his life, sharpen his mind, and figure out how to turn hustle into something stable, structured, and scalable.

I grew up in Detroit, surrounded by real-life problems that didn't come with instruction manuals. I've fought through financial setbacks, family challenges, self-doubt, and seasons where the path forward felt completely unclear. I worked jobs I didn't love, tried businesses that didn't work, and made decisions that cost me time, money, and confidence. I've been discouraged, underestimated, and counted out even by people I thought would support me.

But every struggle became a lesson. Every lesson became a system. And every system became part of what you're holding right now. When I finally decided to stop operating from survival mode and start operating from structure, everything changed. I found clarity in my purpose, confidence in my abilities, and a new level of discipline that turned my setbacks into stepping stones.

The Real Life XP Growth Engine is the blueprint I used to transform my life and business. It's the same framework that took me from uncertainty and inconsistency to making multiple six figures per year, impacting thousands of entrepreneurs along the way.

This volume contains all three parts of the Real Life XP framework:

- **The Seven Pillars** - the mindset, identity, and foundation every entrepreneur needs

- **The Seven Stages of Scaling** - the roadmap that shows exactly where you are and what to do next
- **The Seven Growth Gears** - the levers inside your business you must tune, strengthen, and accelerate to achieve real momentum

These aren't theories. These are the tools I used to rebuild my life from scratch. Everything here was shaped by real experiences, real adversity, and real breakthroughs. I created this because I know what it feels like to want more but not know how to get there. I know what it feels like to start from behind. I know what it feels like to fight battles in silence while still showing up in the world like everything is fine. And I also know what it feels like to win. To break patterns. To outgrow the old version of yourself. To become the leader your business and your life deserves.

If you're reading this, you're not here by accident. You're here because you're ready. Ready to learn. Ready to grow. Ready to build something real.

My only goal with this body of work is simple:
To help you accelerate your progress, avoid my mistakes, and step into the highest-level version of yourself as a business owner and leader.

Welcome to the Real Life XP Growth Engine. Let's build something powerful something you'll be proud of.

– Alvin C. Hill IV, MBA
aka Coach JP

BOOK 1

THE REAL LIFE XP FRAMEWORK

The Seven Pillars of Real Life Exponential Progress

Alvin C. Hill IV, MBA (Coach JP)

TABLE OF CONTENTS

INTRODUCTION

THE ORIGIN OF REAL LIFE XP:

Building a Framework for Entrepreneurs Who Never Had a Blueprint

I didn't set out to create a coaching program. I set out to find answers. Like many entrepreneurs starting from unconventional and disadvantaged circumstances, I did exactly what the online world told me to do: I bought the courses. All of them. Thousands of dollars' worth. Marketing courses. Sales courses. Mindset courses. Branding courses. Automation courses. "Make 6-figures in 60 days" courses.

I consumed them. Studied them. Took notes. Applied what I could. And after all of it, after years of watching experts say the same things in different voices, something hit me: None of these programs talked about what it really takes to start a business as a minority entrepreneur with real responsibilities, real trauma, real bills, real pressure, and a real life.

They were built for people who had support systems, not survival systems. For people who had financial cushions, not financial trauma. For people who could afford to fail quietly, not people whose whole family depended on them getting it right.

They talked about marketing funnels, but not mindset battles. They talked about branding colors, but not childhood wounds. They talked about productivity systems, but not the real distractions that come from living a life with instability. They talked about automation, but not the feeling of doing everything alone. They taught business, but not real life business.

They were speaking a language that didn't match my circumstances or the circumstances of thousands of entrepreneurs like me. So, I realized... If I wanted a framework that fit my reality, I would have to build it myself.

I Spent Years Building the Program I Needed and That So Many Others Needed Too

Real Life XP wasn't created in a weekend. It wasn't inspired by a trend. It wasn't pieced together from other people's content. I built Real Life XP from scratch.

I spent YEARS studying:

- what minority entrepreneurs struggle with
- what entrepreneurs with trauma backgrounds need
- what systems actually produce results
- what real discipline looks like
- what structure does to a chaotic life
- what processes and automation can heal
- what credit and capital can unlock
- how mindset transforms identity
- how leadership creates opportunity
- how legacy gives meaning to struggle

Then I spent another year mapping out the **Seven Pillars** - the full transformation cycle every entrepreneur must go through, in the right order, at the right depth, with the right tools.

These pillars don't teach theory.

They teach survival.
They teach structure.
They teach scaling.
They teach identity-building.
They teach the REAL path to entrepreneurship for real people with real lives.

The Real Life XP Framework wasn't "thought of." It was lived, refined, tested, broken, rebuilt, and perfected.

What "XP" Really Means and Why It Matters to Your Success

XP stands for Exponential Progress.

Why exponential instead of linear? Because linear progress is slow. Linear growth is predictable. Linear thinking is basic. Linear effort is "one foot in front of the other."

And minority entrepreneurs - entrepreneurs with past struggles, entrepreneurs without support networks, entrepreneurs rebuilding their lives - we don't have the luxury of slow, one-step-at-a time progress.

We need transformation, not tiny improvements.
We need breakthroughs, not baby steps.
We need systems, not struggle.
We need strategy, not survival.

Exponential Progress means:

- growing faster because your systems multiply your efforts
- doing more with less because automation works for you
- expanding your capacity because you build teams, not pressure
- scaling intentionally, not emotionally
- compressing years into months through structure and clarity
- building momentum that multiplies itself

This is why Real Life XP is different. It doesn't teach you how to "work harder" - it teaches you how to multiply your effort so you can grow your business at a pace that truly changes your life.

Why Exponential Progress Is Better Than Linear Progress

1. Linear progress depends on YOU doing everything.

Exponential progress depends on SYSTEMS doing the work.

2. Linear progress takes years.

Exponential progress compresses time with automation, delegation, and structure.

3. Linear progress burns you out.

Exponential progress frees you up.

4. Linear progress means learning slow and failing slow.

Exponential progress means learning fast, adjusting fast, and scaling fast.

5. Linear progress is survival.

Exponential progress is strategy.

6. Linear progress keeps you in the hustle.

Exponential progress turns you into a CEO.

7. Linear progress helps you make money for today.

Exponential progress helps you build a legacy for tomorrow.

In the Real Life XP Program, we build businesses that grow even when YOU aren't working. Because exponential progress is the ONLY path that gives minority entrepreneurs:

- time freedom
- financial stability
- scalable structure
- generational opportunity
- and peace

We already survived linear progress in life. XP is about elevating beyond survival.

Who This Book Is For

This book is for the entrepreneur who has grit, fire, and passion but never had a blueprint. It's for the entrepreneur who grew up in circumstances that required strength before structure and now needs both.

It's for the entrepreneur who:

- never had a mentor
- never had guidance
- never had family support
- never had financial help
- never had a safe environment to grow
- never had business role models
- never had someone show them the real path

It's for the entrepreneurs who are:

✓ minority-owned
✓ service-based
✓ ambitious
✓ rebuilding
✓ redefining their lives
✓ breaking generational patterns
✓ starting from pressure, not privilege
✓ determined to change their story
✓ ready to build what their family never had

This book is for YOU.

How the Real Life XP Framework Will Help You?

This framework helps you:

- strengthen your mindset
- structure your business
- build processes that multiply
- use automation to free your time

- access business credit
- secure funding
- build a magnetic brand
- lead a team
- scale responsibly
- build generational wealth
- create a legacy that lasts

This book gives you what all those expensive courses never did:

A complete system for real life entrepreneurship.

- Not theory.
- Not hype.
- Not shortcuts.
- Not recycled tactics.

✓ REAL structure.
✓ REAL action.
✓ REAL clarity.
✓ REAL transformation.

You Are the XP.

Your life is the proof.
Your legacy is the result.

This book isn't just instruction, it's empowerment.
This is the blueprint I wish I had.

The framework I needed.
The structure I built for people like us.

Welcome to the beginning of your exponential transformation.
Welcome to Real Life XP.

CHAPTER 1

PILLAR ONE: MINDSET & MOTIVATION

The Foundation of Every Real Life Success Story

Most entrepreneurs think their problem is money, marketing, or support. But in real life? Your first problem is always you.

Your habits.
Your discipline.
Your emotions.
Your excuses.
Your mindset.
Your identity.

That's why the first pillar of Real Life XP is Mindset & Motivation. Because before your business becomes consistent, you have to become consistent. Before your income grows, you have to grow. Before you scale your structure, you have to scale your character. I learned this the hard way.

Opening Story:

The Discipline That Saved My Life

People see the MBA.
They see the business.
They see the coaching.
They see the confidence.

But they don't see the part of the story built in foster homes, boys' homes, juvenile detention, state and federal prisons. They don't see the nights I had to figure out who I was without support. They don't see the moments I had to make decisions nobody prepared me for. They don't see the days I had to motivate myself to fight for a future nobody believed I would have. Mindset wasn't something I learned from a book, it was something I had to build to survive. But that's the advantage. Because once you've had to depend on your own strength, your own discipline, your own internal engine you realize something:

Nobody can outwork a person who had to grow up early.

- ✓ You know pressure.
- ✓ You know pain.
- ✓ You know perseverance.

What you need now is **structure.**

- Not hype.
- Not fluff.
- Not "motivation."

but the **internal operating system** of a CEO. That's what Mindset & Motivation is about.

Big Idea:

Your Business Will Never Outgrow Your Mentality

Most entrepreneurs don't stall because they lack skills.
They stall because they still think like:

- a hustler,
- a survivor,
- a worker,
- or a person reacting to life instead of directing it.

You cannot scale chaos.
You cannot grow what you won't manage.
You cannot build a business on emotional inconsistency.

Your success is built on:

- how you think,
- how you respond,
- how you lead yourself when nobody's watching,
- and how you show up on the days you don't feel like it.

This is why Mindset & Motivation is Pillar One, because everything else depends on it.

Real Life XP Principle #1:

Identity Creates Direction. Discipline Creates Momentum.

You can have the greatest marketing plan in the world but if you don't follow through? You stay stuck. You can have the best offer in your industry but if you're inconsistent? You stay invisible.

You can have the idea, the talent, the vision but if your habits don't match your goals? You repeat the same month over and over again. Real Life XP begins with transforming your identity:
"Who do I need to become to lead the business I want to build?"

Because when your identity shifts:

- your habits change,
- your expectations rise,
- your standards increase,
- your boundaries strengthen,
- and your business follows your lead.

Framework:

The Real Life XP Mindset Model

1. Clarity → Who You Are

Define your identity. Not based on your past based on your purpose.

2. Discipline → What You Do

Your habits determine your height.

3. Consistency → How You Show Up

The world rewards the person who stays standing.

4. Emotional Mastery → How You React

Pressure will expose your operating system.

5. Vision → Why You Keep Going

When the "why" is strong, the setbacks become steps.

Coach JP Insight (Raw Truth):

Your excuses are more polished than your execution.

Entrepreneurs don't fall behind because of lack of opportunity.
They fall behind because:

- emotions control their effort
- feelings run their schedule
- fear leads their decisions
- laziness hides behind "overwhelm"
- and consistency collapses under pressure

This pillar is designed to rebuild your internal structure so you can operate on command not on mood.

Common Mistakes (XP Corrections)

Mistake 1: You think motivation is the answer

Correction:
Motivation is temporary. Discipline is automatic.

Mistake 2: You blame circumstances

Correction:
Circumstances don't decide outcomes — habits do.

Mistake 3: You wait until you "feel ready"

Correction:
Readiness is built through repetition.

Mistake 4: You think you need confidence first

Correction:
Confidence comes from competence. Competence comes from consistency.

Mistake 5: You treat your business like a side activity

Correction:
You get side results because you think like a side hustler.

Real Life Application (Implementation Steps)

Step 1: Write Your Identity Statement

Who do I need to become to handle the level of business I want?

Step 2: Build Your CEO Routine

Morning + evening routines intentionally designed for clarity and consistency.

Step 3: Create Your "Non-Negotiables List"

These are the habits you commit to daily, no exceptions.

Step 4: Eliminate One Weak Habit

Choose one habit killing your momentum and destroy it systematically.

Step 5: Install Your "Pressure Protocol"

A method for how you respond on your worst days.

Exercises + Worksheets

Exercise 1: The Next-Level Identity Shift

Prompts:

- What version of me is required to hit my next revenue goal?
- What habits does that person have?
- What habits does that person NOT have?
- Who do I need to stop being?

Exercise 2: Trigger Mapping

Identify emotional triggers and build replacement responses.

Exercise 3: The Discipline Audit

What do you do consistently that hurts your business?
What do you do consistently that helps it?

Reflection & Journal Prompts

- When did I let my emotions dictate my effort this month?
- What have I been avoiding, and why?
- What would my next-level self do differently tomorrow?
- What fear is still controlling my decisions?
- What is one lie I keep telling myself?

Closing Motivation

You've survived too much to be inconsistent now. You've fought through things most people would fold under. Mindset is not your weakness; it's your weapon. Now you're learning to sharpen it. This pillar is about building the inner strength required to lead, grow, and scale not just in business, but in life. Because before you build a business… you must build the person who can run it.

CHAPTER 2

PILLAR TWO: BUSINESS FORMATION & SYSTEMS

Turning Hustle Into Structure

Most entrepreneurs don't fail because their idea is bad. They fail because their foundation is weak. If your business was a house, most people are trying to build the roof before they pour the concrete. They want clients before they create a system. They want marketing before they create structure. They want money before they create order. But the truth is simple:

- **You cannot scale disorder.**
- **You cannot grow what you cannot manage.**
- **You cannot lead what you have not structured.**

This is why full-time entrepreneurs burn out, and why side-hustlers never break into real revenue. They're building on chaos instead of a foundation. Pillar Two exists to fix that. This pillar is where you stop "winging it" and become a real CEO.

Opening Story:

The Day I Realized Hustle Wasn't Enough

There was a moment early in my entrepreneurial journey that shifted everything. I was grinding hard late nights, heavy pressure, no sleep. Money was coming in, but so were the problems.

Clients weren't organized. My schedule was out of control. People were calling me all day.

Invoices were late. Systems didn't exist. And everything depended on me. I wasn't running my business. I was holding it together with duct tape and adrenaline.

One day, after a long week filled with mistakes, missed opportunities, and frustration, I said to myself:

"I don't have a business.
I have a job I created for myself."

That's when it hit me. Hustle might get you started, but it will never take you to the next level. What saved me wasn't working harder, it was working **organized**. Documenting processes. Creating structure. Building systems. Getting disciplined.

This is what leveled up my business. This is what allowed me to coach others. This is what allowed me to scale Real Life Business Solutions. And this is the transformation you're about to make.

Big Idea:

Structure Creates Freedom

People think structure limits them. The truth? Structure is what finally sets you free.

When your business is properly formed and systemized:

- You stop guessing
- You stop stressing
- You stop starting over
- You stop drowning in tasks
- You stop putting out fires
- You stop being the bottleneck

And you start:

✓ Moving with clarity

- ✓ Feeling confident in your operations
- ✓ Creating smooth client experiences
- ✓ Working predictable hours
- ✓ Running your business like a CEO
- ✓ Earning more without working more

Systems give you your life back. This pillar is where you evolve from a hustler into a business owner and eventually into a leader.

Real Life XP Principle #2:

If You Don't Build Systems, Your Problems Will Build Themselves.

Lack of structure always becomes:

- missed payments
- customer complaints
- confusion
- overwhelm
- burnout
- bad reviews
- inconsistent income
- mental exhaustion

Entrepreneurs who scale successfully don't rely on memory, vibes, luck, or momentum. They rely on systems. Systems that tell them:

- what to do
- when to do it
- how to do it
- who should do it
- what tools support it
- and what outcome is expected

Consistency is not a personality trait. It's a system. Structure is not extra work. It's the backbone of your future success.

Framework:

The Real Life XP Business Foundation Model

These are the six components required before you scale:

1. Legal & Structural Setup

- Register your business (LLC, S-Corp when appropriate)
- Obtain EIN
- Open business bank account
- Set up bookkeeping
- Get proper licensing
- Secure insurance
- Establish business address, phone, email, website

If you miss this step, funding becomes impossible and credibility collapses.

2. Business Credibility Checklist

This is what lenders, partners, and clients look for:

- Consistent branding across platforms
- Professional website
- CRM set up
- Payment system
- Scheduling system
- Policies and contract templates
- Google Business Profile

This positions you as legitimate not amateur.

3. Operational Systems

Every business needs systems for:

- Lead tracking
- Sales follow-up
- Client onboarding
- Service delivery
- Client support

- Billing & collections
- Reporting
- Team communication

Without these systems, you work harder but grow slower.

4. Standard Operating Procedures (SOPs)

Your business must be documentable. Every recurring task should be written as:

1. Purpose
2. Steps
3. Tools needed
4. Expected outcome

If you can't teach someone else to do it, you don't own a business you own a task.

5. Technology & Automation

This is where your business becomes efficient:

- CRM
- Email automation
- Text automation
- Scheduling automation
- Pipeline tracking
- Contract and invoice automation
- Onboarding sequences
- Task management tools

Technology is not a luxury, it's leverage.

6. Daily, Weekly, and Monthly Operations Rhythm

Routine is the heartbeat of your business.

- **Daily**: revenue-producing activities
- **Weekly**: reviews, follow-ups, marketing
- **Monthly**: finances, tracking metrics, goals

If you don't have a rhythm, you don't have a business you have chaos.

Coach JP Insight (Raw Truth):

You're overworked because your business is under-structured.

The reason you're stressed isn't because you don't have help. It's because you don't have organization. Most entrepreneurs think: "I need a team." No. You need a system. A system you can plug people into. If you hire people before you build structure, they will drown in your disorganization. You don't scale people you scale systems.

Common Mistakes (XP Corrections)

Mistake 1: Starting with marketing before having systems

Correction:
Traffic without structure creates overwhelm.

Mistake 2: Running everything through memory

Correction:
The brain is for thinking, not for storage.

Mistake 3: Doing everything manually

Correction:
If you can automate it, you must automate it.

Mistake 4: Not documenting processes

Correction:
What's not documented cannot be delegated.

Mistake 5: Treating the business like a side project

Correction:
Professional structure leads to professional results.

Real Life Application (Implementation Steps)

Step 1: Complete Your Business Credibility Setup

This includes all legal, structural, and brand consistency items.

Step 2: Build Your Core Systems

- CRM
- Payment platform
- Scheduling tool
- Onboarding process
- Communication system

Step 3: Map Your Operations Flow

From lead → to client → to fulfillment → to retention.

Step 4: Create Your First SOP

Pick one repeated task and fully document it.

Step 5: Automate One Pain Point

Follow-ups, onboarding, scheduling, etc.

Exercises + Worksheets

Exercise 1: Operations Flow Mapping

Draw your entire process from first contact to end result.

Exercise 2: System Gap Audit

Identify every missing system slowing down your business.

Exercise 3: Weekly CEO Schedule Creation

Design a weekly routine that will run your business consistently.

Reflection & Journal Prompts

- Where am I still operating like a hustler instead of a CEO?
- What part of my business feels the most chaotic, and why?
- What system would change my life if it was built today?
- What process do I need to document immediately?
- If someone took over my business tomorrow, what would they need to know?

Closing Motivation

Systems aren't just about making your business run smoother, they're about protecting your future. You didn't come this far to stay overwhelmed. You didn't survive what you survived just to work without order. You didn't build a vision just to hold it together with stress. This pillar transforms you from a hustler into a builder. A builder into a leader. And a leader into someone capable of scaling something real. This is where your business becomes official. This is where structure replaces struggle. This is where chaos ends and clarity begins.

CHAPTER 3
PILLAR THREE: PROCESS & AUTOMATION

Build Systems That Run Even When Life Gets Real

Let me be honest with you. Most entrepreneurs don't have a business problem; they have a repetition problem. They're doing the same tasks over and over.

Manually.
Emotionally.
Exhaustingly.

They're sending the same messages. Following up with the same clients. Fixing the same issues. Answering the same questions. Rebuilding the same processes every week. It's not the work that stresses them, it's the fact that everything requires their hands, their memory, their energy.

That's not a business.
That's a burnout program.

Process & Automation exists to fix that. This pillar transforms your business into a machine one that works even on your worst day, even when life gets unpredictable, even when you're tired, busy, sick, or overwhelmed. This pillar is the secret to freedom.

Opening Story:

The Week That Forced Me into Automation

I remember a week where everything hit at once: business, kids, real life, emergencies, everything. My phone was blowing up. Clients needed updates. Leads needed follow-ups. Invoices needed sending. People were texting me at all hours. I was juggling calls, emails, tasks, and problems. On Wednesday, I sat at my desk and realized something:

I built a business that can't run if I'm not running.

Not because I didn't have the skills, but because I didn't have the systems. That day, something snapped inside me in a good way. I said: Never again will my business collapse because I'm human. And that's when automation became my non-negotiable.

I automated onboarding.
I automated follow-ups.
I automated scheduling.
I automated reminders.
I automated status updates.
I automated my pipeline.

And slowly, everything changed.

Stress disappeared.
Clarity increased.
Consistency improved.
Revenue stabilized.
And life became manageable.

Process & Automation didn't just save my business it saved my peace.

Big Idea:

Automation Creates Consistency and Consistency Creates Cash Flow

Entrepreneurs love to say:

- "I need more time."
- "I need more help."
- "I need more support."

But what they really need is:

- **Fewer manual tasks**
- **Fewer repeated conversations**
- **Fewer emotional decisions**
- **Fewer points of failure**
- **More predictable systems**

Automation isn't about replacing human connection, it's about replacing human burden. Your time should be spent thinking, leading, creating, and selling not repeating the same 25 administrative tasks every day. Process & Automation allows you to:

- Get more done in less time
- Reduce mistakes
- Increase professionalism
- Improve client experience
- Scale without stress
- Prevent burnout
- Grow without needing a bigger team immediately
- Move like a real CEO

This pillar is non-negotiable if you want stability AND scale.

Real Life XP Principle #3:

Whatever you have to do more than twice should be automated or documented.

1. If you repeat it - automate it.
2. If someone else will need to do it - document, it.
3. If it eats your time - systemize it.

Entrepreneurs stay stuck because they are emotionally attached to doing everything themselves. They confuse activity with progress. They confuse busyness with productivity. But here's the truth: You are not paid for the tasks you repeat, you are paid for the value you create. Automation frees you to create value.

Framework:

The Real Life XP Process Automation System (PAS)

This system has 5 parts:

1. Map Your Entire Journey (From Lead to Legacy)

Break your business into steps.

a. **Lead Stage**
   How do people find you?
b. **Nurture Stage**
   How do you build trust?
c. **Sales Stage**
   How do you convert?
d. **Onboarding Stage**
   How do you welcome clients?
e. **Fulfillment Stage**
   How do you deliver the service?
f. **Retention Stage**
   How do you keep clients longer?

g. **Expansion Stage**
How do you upsell or ascend clients?

Everything should be a mapped process, not a memory.

2. Identify Bottlenecks

These are the things slowing your business down.

Common bottlenecks:

- Late follow-ups
- Missed appointments
- Manual onboarding
- Repeated questions
- Forgotten tasks
- Delayed payments
- Confusing workflows
- Too many steps
- No CRM
- Disorganized communication

Your business is only as fast as your slowest system.

3. Automate Routine Tasks

Automation replaces repetitive work.

Automate:

- Follow-ups
- Appointment reminders
- Lead nurturing
- New lead notifications
- Payment reminders
- Contract sending
- Onboarding emails
- File requests
- Surveys and feedback
- Upsell offers

Every time you automate something, you reclaim your time.

4. Create SOPs (Standard Operating Procedures)

SOPs turn chaos into clarity.

Every SOP should include:

- **Purpose**:(why the task matters)
- **Steps:** (in order, with screenshots when needed)
- **Tools:** (software or resources)
- **Expected outcome:** (what "done" looks like)

This turns your business into a machine.

5. Assign Ownership

Systems run the business. People run the systems.

Everyone must know:

- What they own
- When they do it
- How they do it
- What tools they use
- What results they must produce

Ownership creates accountability. Accountability creates growth.

Coach JP Insight (Raw Truth):

Your business is falling apart because too much depends on you.

You're the CEO, the assistant, the tech support, the salesperson, the marketer, the bookkeeper, and the operations manager.

That's why you feel overwhelmed.

You don't need more days.

You need fewer tasks.

You don't need more help.

You need more automation.

You don't need more willpower.

You need more structure.

Automation is not a luxury, it's survival.

Common Mistakes (XP Corrections)

Mistake 1: Doing everything manually

Correction:
Automate what you repeat.

Mistake 2: Trying to scale chaos

Correction:
Systemize before you multiply.

Mistake 3: Thinking automation is "too techy"

Correction:
Every tool you need is user-friendly today.

Mistake 4: Relying on memory instead of process

Correction:
Memory breaks - systems don't.

Mistake 5: Not onboarding clients with structure

Correction:
A smooth start prevents a messy experience.

Real Life Application (Implementation Steps)

Step 1: Build Your Business Map

Map every step of your client journey.

Step 2: Choose 3 Tasks to Automate This Week

Pick the tasks you repeat the most.

Step 3: Build Your First Workflow

Examples:

- Lead follow-up
- Appointment reminders
- Client onboarding
- Payment reminders

Step 4: Create Your First SOP Document

Pick a task you want to delegate.

Step 5: Standardize Your Communications

Scripts, templates, and automated messages.

Exercises + Worksheets

Exercise 1: The "Three Repeats" Rule

List every task you repeated this week. If it happened 3+ times, it needs automation.

Exercise 2: Journey Mapping Diagram

Draw out your entire process visually.

Exercise 3: Automation Identification

Highlight every step that can be automated or delegated.

Exercise 4: SOP Creation Template

Fill in:

- Task Name
- Purpose
- Trigger (when the task starts)
- Steps
- Tools
- Expected Outcome

Reflection & Journal Prompts

- What are the top 5 tasks draining my energy?
- How much time do I waste on manual work?
- What parts of my business collapse when I'm tired or unavailable?
- What would my business look like if everything were automated?
- Am I running my business or is it running me?

Closing Motivation

- You didn't build your dream just to drown in tasks.
- You didn't survive what you survived just to be overwhelmed every day.
- You didn't fight through your past to be trapped in your present.

Automation is not about technology it's about liberation.

This pillar gives you your life back.

Your time back.
Your clarity back.
Your peace back.

You deserve to run a business that works for you, not against you. You deserve systems that help you win even when life gets real.

This is where you stop being the engine and become the architect.

You're building a machine now.

A real business.
A scalable business.
A predictable business.

This is where freedom begins.

CHAPTER 4

PILLAR FOUR: CREDIT & CAPITAL

Fuel for the Business You're Building

Let me make this as real as possible: Most minority entrepreneurs don't fail because they lack the talent. They fail because they lack the funding. They had the vision, but couldn't finance the vision. They had the skills but didn't have the structure to access capital. They had the hustle but didn't have the credit to scale the hustle into a business.

And I want you to feel this:

Your dream doesn't just need belief. It needs backing.

- You can't scale on sweat alone.
- You can't fund growth on emotions.
- You can't hire on hope.
- You can't expand on empty pockets.

Every successful business you see today, every brand, every franchise, every tech startup, every empire had ACCESS.

✓ Access to credit.
✓ Access to capital.
✓ Access to leverage.
✓ Access to systems.

You don't have to be born with it. You can build it. This is the pillar that makes your business financially unstoppable.

Opening Story:

When My Personal Money Couldn't Carry My Business Anymore

I used to believe I could "out-hustle" any financial problem. If money got tight? Work harder. If bills were due? Work harder. If equipment broke? Work harder.

But the truth hit me one day when the business had expenses I couldn't cover instantly:

- Software fees
- Marketing costs
- Hiring support
- Taxes
- Unexpected repairs
- Growth investments

I realized I was trying to run a business with the same financial tools I used to survive growing up, cash and hope. That day, I decided: "I will NEVER let lack of capital be the reason my business doesn't grow."

And I rebuilt everything:

- My personal credit
- My business structure
- My financial systems
- My access to lines of credit
- My readiness for funding
- My relationship with money mindset

The day my business got its first approval for a credit line, something inside me shifted. Not because of the money but because of the power. I finally had OPTIONS. And options give an entrepreneur freedom.

Big Idea:

Your Business Must Outgrow Your Personal Wallet

If your business depends on your personal cash, your personal emotion, your personal credit score, or your personal bank account, you don't have a business, you have a financial liability. Entrepreneurs get stuck because:

- They can't afford ads
- They can't afford help
- They can't afford systems
- They can't afford growth
- They can't afford mistakes
- They can't afford slow months

All because they're funding a business from their personal life.

That's not sustainable.
That's not scalable.
That's not strategic.

Credit & Capital gives you the financial backbone you need to grow with confidence and intention.

Real Life XP Principle #4:

Credit Is Not Debt, It's Leverage.

Capital Is Not Stress. It's Strategy. People fear credit because they've only experienced consumer credit.

Swipe it.
Pay it later.
Get into a hole.
Repeat.

But business credit?
It's different.
It's strategic.
It's intentional.

And it's designed to help you grow.

Business credit exists so you can:

- Invest in marketing
- Hire team members
- Manage cash flow
- Buy equipment
- Upgrade operations
- Expand locations
- Launch products
- Survive slow seasons
- Increase your capacity

And the best part?

It's not connected to your personal life.

- Your personal credit becomes protected.
- Your personal money stays safe.
- Your business stands on its own feet.

This is how real companies scale.
And now it's your turn.

Framework:

The Real Life XP Credit & Capital System

This system has 5 major components:

1. Business Credibility Setup (The Non-Negotiables)

Lenders want to see a real business not a hustle.

You need:

- Proper entity structure (LLC or Corp)
- EIN
- Business bank account
- Business email

- Professional website
- Business phone
- Google Business Profile
- Matching business information everywhere
- Operating Agreements
- Licenses/Permits
- Bookkeeping system

This is your financial identity. If this is not right, credit is impossible.

2. Personal Credit Rehab (If Needed)

Before you get business credit, you need personal credit **clean** enough to be taken seriously. You don't need a perfect score. You need a functional one.

Key focuses:

- Reduce utilization
- Remove negative items
- Add positive accounts
- Build payment history
- Keep credit clean and calm

Lenders use your personal credit to trust your business creditworthiness temporarily. Once you're in the system, business credit stands alone.

3. Business Credit Building (Tiered Approach)

Business credit builds step-by-step.

Tier 1: Vendor Accounts (Net 30/60)

Examples:

- Grainger
- Uline
- Summa Office Supplies
- Shirtsy (reporting vendors only)
- Nav

These accounts help you build your business credit score (PAYDEX).

Tier 2: Store Credit Accounts

Examples:

- Amazon Business
- Home Depot
- Lowe's
- Best Buy

These come after 3–6 months of responsible vendor usage.

Tier 3: Revolving Business Credit

Examples:

- Fuel cards
- Visa lines
- MasterCard business cards
- Tier 3–4 corporate accounts

Tier 4: High-Limit Business Credit

This includes:

- $10K–$100K lines of credit
- Business loans
- Equipment financing
- Invoice factoring
- SBA loans

This is where real scaling happens.

4. Funding Strategy

Once you're credible, lenders want to give you money.

Funding options include:

- Traditional loans
- Business credit cards
- Business lines of credit
- Revolving credit
- Term loans

- Equipment financing
- Merchant cash advances (last resort)
- Grants
- Community lending
- Peer-to-peer lending
- SBA funding

Each serves a different purpose. This chapter helps you choose wisely.

5. Financial Management System (The XP Money Map)

You need a rhythm.

Daily

- Revenue tracking
- Transaction checking

Weekly

- Invoices
- Collections
- Expense review

Monthly

- Profit review
- Cash-flow planning
- KPI review
- Tax preparation

This keeps your financial foundation strong.

Coach JP Insight (Raw Truth):

You're not lacking funding, you're lacking structure. Lenders WANT to give money to structured businesses. They WANT to invest in organized entrepreneurs. They WANT to approve applications for people who operate on paper like a real company.

But most entrepreneurs look like:

- A side hustle
- A passion project
- A part-time dream
- A financially unstable operation
- A business with no documentation or credibility

You're not getting denied because you're not good enough. You're getting denied because your business isn't organized enough. Once you fix that? Doors open everywhere.

Common Mistakes (XP Corrections)

Mistake 1: Using personal credit for business expenses

Correction:
Separate your life from your business.

Mistake 2: Thinking credit is "bad"

Correction:
Credit is leverage, not debt.

Mistake 3: Applying for funding too early

Correction:
Build credibility first.

Mistake 4: Mixing business and personal accounts

Correction:
Separate everything.

Mistake 5: Believing your income is too small to get funding

Correction:
Lenders approve structure, not size.

Real Life Application (Implementation Steps)

Step 1: Complete Your Business Credibility Checklist

Every detail must match everywhere.

Step 2: Check Personal Credit for Readiness

If needed, repair and rebuild.

Step 3: Apply for Tier 1 Vendor Accounts

Start the business credit file.

Step 4: Build 3–6 Months of Payment History

Fast payments = high PAYDEX score.

Step 5: Begin Tier 2 and Tier 3 Accounts

Scale your credit power.

Step 6: Create a Funding Plan

Identify the type of capital your business will need in 6–12 months.

Exercises + Worksheets

Exercise 1: Financial Identity Assessment

List everything your business is missing structurally.

Exercise 2: Credit Health Snapshot

Evaluate:

- Score
- Utilization
- Inquiries
- Payment history
- Negative items

Exercise 3: Business Credit Starter Plan

Choose your first 3–5 net-30 accounts.

Exercise 4: Funding Vision Worksheet

Write down:

- What you want to fund?
- Why you need it?
- How much will be required?
- What category of funding suits your goals?

Reflection & Journal Prompts

- What is my current relationship with money?
- What fears do I have around funding and credit?
- How would my business change with $50K available?
- What beliefs from my past are limiting my financial future?
- What would real financial freedom look like to me?

Closing Motivation

You didn't come this far to let money stop you now. You didn't survive your past to remain financially handcuffed. You didn't beat the statistics to run a business that's always one slow month away from collapse.

This pillar puts power in your hands.

It gives you access.
It gives you leverage.
It gives you freedom.
It gives you options.

Because the truth is this: Credit & Capital is not about money it's about the future you're building. And now, you're building it with intention.

CHAPTER 5

PILLAR FIVE: MARKETING & BRANDING

Become Seen. Become Heard. Become Chosen.

Let's get straight to it: Most entrepreneurs don't have a talent problem they have an attention problem.

You're good at what you do.
You solve real problems.
You bring real value.
You've put in the work.
You've survived real life and turned it into purpose.

But the world doesn't reward the best-kept secret.

If people don't SEE you
If people don't HEAR you
If people don't KNOW you exist
If people don't FEEL your message

They can't choose you.

Marketing & Branding is the pillar that makes your business louder, clearer, more credible, and more magnetic. This is where your message becomes a movement. This is where your brand becomes a force. This is where you start attracting the customers meant for you. You don't need 100,000 followers. You need the right people paying attention to the right message. And once you learn to control attention? Your business becomes unstoppable.

Opening Story:

The Moment I Realized People Weren't Ignoring Me They Just Didn't Know Me

There was a time when I thought people weren't supporting my business because they didn't care. I'd post something. Get a couple likes. One comment if I was lucky. Crickets. Meanwhile, I was giving people VALUE. I was showing up. I was working. In my mind, the problem was the audience. But one day it hit me:

- It's not that people weren't supporting me.
- It's that they didn't really SEE me.
- They didn't know me.
- They didn't understand me.
- They didn't feel connected to me.
- I wasn't visible.
- I wasn't clear.
- I wasn't branded.
- I wasn't marketing with purpose.
- I was posting not positioning.
- I was talking not communicating.
- I was active not strategic.

That day, I made a decision: "I will become undeniable."

- ✓ I studied branding.
- ✓ I learned messaging.
- ✓ I built a content rhythm.
- ✓ I told my story.
- ✓ I clarified my voice.
- ✓ I built my brand identity.
- ✓ I marketed consistently and intentionally.

Everything changed.

People began reaching out. Clients started signing up. My message started spreading. Opportunities started coming. The brand became magnetic. Marketing didn't just grow my business, it grew my impact.

Big Idea:

Branding Is Who You Are.

Marketing Is How People Find Out.

Branding = Identity
Marketing = Attention

Branding is the meaning behind your business.
Marketing is the movement behind your message.

Branding is your presence.
Marketing is your promotion.

Branding is how people remember you.
Marketing is how people discover you.

Branding answers:

- Who are you?
- What do you stand for?
- What problem do you solve?
- Why should people trust you?
- How are you different?

Marketing answers:

- Where are your people?
- How do you reach them?
- What attracts them?
- What makes them stop scrolling?
- What makes them want to learn more?

When these two pillars come together, your business becomes magnetic.

Real Life XP Principle #5:

Visibility Creates Opportunity. Positioning Creates Demand. Branding Creates Trust.

This is the formula. Most people are out here trying to "be consistent" without being strategic.

- You don't need more posts.
- You need more purpose.
- You don't need more videos.
- You need more messaging.
- You don't need more content.
- You need more clarity.
- Your brand must speak before you do.
- Your reputation must be marketed before you show up.
- Your message must move before you DM anybody.

This is how Real Life XP teaches marketing not as a tactic, but as a skillset that transforms your business forever.

Framework:

The Real Life XP Marketing & Branding Blueprint

This blueprint has 5 components:

1. The Messenger (YOU)

- Your story.
- Your voice.
- Your transformation.
- Your perspective.
- Your personality.
- Your authenticity.

People don't connect to logos they connect to leaders.

Your story is your superpower.
Your transparency is your trust builder.
Your authenticity is your magnet.

2. The Message (WHAT YOU SAY)

Your message must be:

- Clear
- Consistent
- Compelling
- Emotional
- Problem-solving
- Audience-centered

If your message is confusing, you'll lose people.
If your message is generic, you'll blend in.
If your message is powerful, you'll dominate.

3. The Market (WHO YOU SERVE)

You must know:

- Their fears
- Their frustrations
- Their desires
- Their dreams
- Their goals
- Their pain points
- Their limitations
- Their language

If you try to speak to everyone, you speak to no one. When you speak directly to the right people, they feel chosen and they CHOOSE you.

4. The Method (HOW YOU ATTRACT)

Your marketing engine includes:

- Content

- Social media
- Email marketing
- Short-form videos
- Paid ads
- Live events/webinars
- Partnerships
- SEO
- Community
- Storytelling
- Lead magnets
- Funnels

You don't need all of these. You need the RIGHT ones for your business.

5. The Magnet (WHY PEOPLE CHOOSE YOU)

This is the soul of your brand:

- What makes you different
- What you consistently deliver
- How do you transform people
- What people feel when they work with you
- Your culture
- Your promise
- Your reputation
- Your aesthetic
- Your leadership

When people can FEEL your brand, they want to be a part of it.

Coach JP Insight (Raw Truth):

Your brand is not weak, your communication is. You're powerful. You've survived things most people can't imagine. Your life is a story of resilience, discipline, and purpose. But if people can't HEAR that story, if people can't FEEL that message, if people can't SEE that identity. Your brand remains silent. And silent businesses die.

You must become louder.
Clearer.
More intentional.
More expressive.
More consistent.
Bolder.
More YOU.

Your future depends on your visibility.

Common Mistakes (XP Corrections)

Mistake 1: Posting without strategy

Correction:
Build a content system, not random activity.

Mistake 2: Hiding your story

Correction:
Your story is your advantage.

Mistake 3: Trying to be too "professional"

Correction:
Authenticity beats perfection every time.

Mistake 4: Talking about features instead of transformation

Correction:
Clients buy RESULTS, not tools.

Mistake 5: Giving up on marketing too soon

Correction:
Brand recognition takes time. Stay consistent.

Real Life Application (Implementation Steps)

Step 1: Identify Your Core Brand Message

Answer: "What do I want my name to stand for?"

Step 2: Define Your Core Audience

Describe:

- Their problems
- Their fears
- Their desires
- Their goals

Step 3: Create Your Content Pillars

Choose 3–5 topics you'll talk about consistently.

Step 4: Implement a Weekly Content Rhythm

Example:

- Motivation Monday
- Teaching Tuesday
- Storytime Wednesday
- Testimonial Thursday
- Funnel Friday

Step 5: Build Your Visibility System

Choose 2–3 platforms to dominate.

Exercises + Worksheets

Exercise 1: The Brand Identity Audit

Write what your brand stands for in one sentence.

Exercise 2: The Ideal Client Profile

Describe your client in detail.

Exercise 3: Story Vault Creation

List 10 stories from your life that shaped who you are.

Exercise 4: Messaging Clarity Template

Answer:

- What problem do I solve?
- Who do I solve it for?
- Why am I the best person to solve it?
- What makes my approach different?

Reflection & Journal Prompts

- What part of my story am I avoiding sharing?
- What message do I want to be known for?
- What fear is holding me back from being more visible?
- How do I want people to feel when they encounter my brand?
- What would a consistent marketing version of me look like?

Closing Motivation

You were not put on this earth to stay hidden.
You were not built for silence.
You were not meant to be overlooked.
Your story deserves to be heard.
Your brand deserves to be seen.
Your business deserves to be chosen.

Marketing & Branding turn your presence into power, your message into momentum, your identity into influence.

This is where your voice becomes your vehicle.
This is where your brand becomes your bridge.
This is where your story becomes someone else's solution.

You are not invisible, you just haven't activated your spotlight. Now it's time.

CHAPTER 6

PILLAR SIX: LEADERSHIP & TEAM BUILDING

You Can Hustle Alone But You Can't Scale Alone

There is a moment every entrepreneur hits when the grind stops being impressive and starts becoming impossible.

You've pushed.
You've sacrificed.
You've carried the weight.
You've done everything on your own. And honestly...

That's probably how you survived the first phase of your life. You learned to depend on yourself because nobody else showed up. You built resilience because life didn't give you a choice. You became your own leader because you didn't have one. But entrepreneurship will test your independence in a new way.

At some point, your dream will become bigger than your capacity. Your vision will outgrow your schedule. Your business will outpace your energy. Your opportunity will require more than your two hands. And that moment reveals a truth: The greatest barrier to scaling is trying to do everything alone. Leadership & Team Building is where you stop being the only engine and start becoming the architect of a real organization. This pillar transforms you from a solo hustler into a CEO.

Opening Story:

The First Time I Tried to Build a Team and Failed Miserably

I'll be real with you. The first time I tried to hire help, I failed. Not because the people were bad but because **I was not ready to lead them**.

I didn't communicate clearly.
I didn't document anything.
I didn't set expectations.
I didn't delegate correctly.
I didn't know how to give feedback.
I didn't have the patience to teach.
I didn't have the systems for someone else to follow.
I didn't understand how to shift from doing… to leading.

At that time, leadership felt like extra work.

It felt slower.
It felt messy.
It felt uncomfortable.

So, you know what I did? I took everything back. I kept doing it all myself. And for a while, that felt "easier." But it wasn't easier.

It was expensive.
It was exhausting.
It was limiting.
It was unsustainable.

And one day I said: "I can't keep being the reason my business can't grow."

Leadership wasn't optional it was required. From that moment, I learned the skills, systems, and emotional discipline to become the kind of leader people will follow.

Everything changed.

My time expanded.
My business duplicated.
My impact increased.

My systems strengthened.
My capacity exploded.

This pillar will help you do the same.

Big Idea:

Leaders Don't Add Pressure - They Create Structure

People misunderstand leadership. They think leadership is:

- being the boss
- giving orders
- having authority
- being in control
- being the one who knows everything

Leadership isn't any of that.

- ✓ Leadership is clarity.
- ✓ Leadership is influence.
- ✓ Leadership is responsibility.
- ✓ Leadership is alignment.
- ✓ Leadership is communication.
- ✓ Leadership is duplication.
- ✓ Leadership is vision.

Leadership isn't about being in front, it's about bringing people with you. The most successful CEOs aren't the ones who do the most. They're the ones who create systems where others can do their best.

Real Life XP Principle #6:

If everything depends on you, you don't have a business you have a burden.

Let that sink in. If your business breaks when:

- you're tired
- you're sick

- you're busy
- you're overwhelmed
- you're unavailable
- you're behind
- you're traveling

then you don't have a business. You have a time bomb. Leadership multiplies you. It turns your vision into a vehicle other people can drive. It turns your process into a playbook other people can follow. It turns your business into something bigger than your capacity.

Framework:

The Real Life XP Leadership System

This system has 5 core components:

1. Lead Yourself First

You cannot lead others into places you won't go yourself. Self-leadership requires:

- consistency
- emotional control
- discipline
- communication
- time management
- self-awareness
- humility
- accountability

If your team sees you lead yourself, they will trust you to lead them.

2. Clarify the Vision

Your team needs to know:

- Where you're going
- Why you're going there
- What the mission is
- What success looks like

- What the standards are
- How they fit into the journey
- What their role creates

People don't follow tasks they follow purpose.

3. Build Roles, Not Jobs

A "job" is a list of things to do.
A role is a piece of the mission you're trusting someone to own.

Roles require:

- Title
- Purpose
- Responsibilities
- KPIs (metrics)
- Tools
- Processes
- Expected outcomes
- Communication rhythms

When roles are clear, teams are strong.

4. Delegate the Right Way

Delegation isn't: "Can you do this real quick?" That's dumping. Dumping creates chaos.

The Real Life XP Delegation Method:

1. Explain the Why
2. Explain the Outcome
3. Show the Process
4. Give the Tools
5. Give the Deadline
6. Check for Understanding
7. Review at the End
8. Refine Together

This creates ownership, not confusion.

5. Build a Culture of Accountability

People don't rise to your goals. They rise to your standards. Strong teams have:

- weekly check-ins
- daily communication
- monthly reviews
- clear KPIs
- open feedback
- real consequences
- measurable progress

Culture isn't what you say. It's what you tolerate.

Coach JP Insight (Raw Truth):

Your business can't grow because you are holding the door closed.

- You're scared to let go.
- You're scared to trust.
- You're scared someone will mess it up.
- You're scared of repeating old traumas.
- You're scared of depending on people again.
- You're scared of not being in control.

But hear me: **You cannot heal from isolation and scale alone at the same time.**

- You deserve a team that supports you
- You deserve people who help carry the load.
- You deserve systems that make your life easier.
- You deserve structure that multiplies your vision.

Leadership is not losing control. Leadership is gaining help.

Common Mistakes (XP Corrections)

Mistake 1: Hiring too early

Correction:
Build systems BEFORE people.

Mistake 2: Hiring out of desperation

Correction:
Hire from a plan, not a panic.

Mistake 3: Not documenting processes

Correction:
If you can't teach it, you can't delegate it.

Mistake 4: Doing "half-delegation"

Correction:
Delegate the whole task, not pieces.

Mistake 5: Expecting people to read your mind

Correction:
Clarity is your responsibility.

Real Life Application (Implementation Steps)

Step 1: Identify Your First or Next Role

Write a role description with:

- Purpose
- Responsibilities
- KPIs
- Tools
- Success indicators

Step 2: Create Your Leadership Code

Write how you lead and what you expect.

Step 3: Build a Weekly Leadership Rhythm

Examples:

- Monday: Team check-in
- Wednesday: Progress review
- Friday: Performance reflection

Step 4: Document a Process You Will Delegate

Pick one recurring task and build an SOP.

Step 5: Hold One Leadership Conversation

Set expectations clearly and directly.

Exercises + Worksheets

Exercise 1: Leadership Identity Assessment

Ask yourself:

- How do I show up as a leader?
- What do I model?
- What do I tolerate?
- What do I avoid?

Exercise 2: Team Vision Blueprint

Write: What kind of team do I want to build and why?

Exercise 3: The Delegation Playbook

Document:

- The task
- The purpose
- The process
- The tools
- The deadline

Exercise 4: Accountability System Builder

Create simple KPIs for each team member.

Reflection & Journal Prompts

- What scares me most about leading others?
- What part of leadership feels unfamiliar or uncomfortable?
- Who was the best leader I ever had and why?
- What kind of leader do I want to be remembered as?
- What would my business look like with a strong team behind me?

Closing Motivation

You were never meant to build everything alone.
You were never meant to carry the entire vision by yourself.
You were never meant to stay in survival mode forever.

Leadership is your next level. Team building is your next breakthrough. Collaboration is your next elevation. This pillar transforms you from a hustler to a builder to a leader to a CEO. Because the truth is this: You can go fast alone, but you can only go far with a team. This pillar prepares you to go far.

CHAPTER 7

PILLAR SEVEN: LEGACY & IMPACT

Build Something That Outlives You

There comes a moment in every entrepreneur's journey where the goal stops being money and starts being meaning. Where the focus shifts from survival to significance. Where the vision expands beyond today and starts reaching into tomorrow.

That moment that shift is the birth of legacy.

- Legacy is not about being famous.
- Legacy is not about being perfect.
- Legacy is not about pretending your life was easy.

✓ Legacy is about leaving the world different because you were here.
✓ Legacy is about building something that continues after you stop working.
✓ Legacy is about creating opportunities for the next generation.
✓ Legacy is about turning your pain into wisdom someone else can use.
✓ Legacy is about taking what life gave you good or bad and turning it into something powerful.

This pillar transforms your business from a source of income into a source of influence. And influence outlives you.

Opening Story:

When I Realized My Life Was Bigger Than My Pain

There was a moment, a quiet moment, where everything hit me. I started thinking about the people who weren't there for me.

The places I grew up in.
The systems I had to fight against.
The mistakes I made.
The nights I spent alone.
The days I felt forgotten.
The years I spent trying to figure out life on my own.

I thought about the challenges, the trauma, the environment, the lack of guidance, the lack of opportunity, the lack of structure, the lack of direction, the lack of everything a kid should have. And then it hit me:

"Everything I went through wasn't meant to break me. It was meant to build someone else."

My story wasn't just mine; it was a blueprint.

A roadmap.
A testimony.
A guide for people coming behind me.
A message for people who needed to hear it.
A warning for people who didn't know.
A light for people still walking in the dark.

That day, I knew:

My life wasn't about what I survived. It was about what I could do to help others survive. That is legacy. That is impact. That is why this pillar exists.

Big Idea:

Income Pays the Bills.

Impact Pays It Forward.

Money is important.
Financial freedom is essential.
Scaling matters.
Growth matters.
Abundance matters.

But legacy? Legacy makes everything meaningful.

Legacy means:

- Your business outlives your energy
- Your story outlives your struggle
- Your wisdom outlives your mistakes
- Your lessons outlive your lifetime
- The next generation gets to start where you finished
- You didn't walk through fire for nothing
- Your journey becomes someone else's elevation

Legacy is long-term impact, not short-term income. Impact is purpose in action.

Real Life XP Principle #7:

Legacy is not built by accident.

It's built by intention. People think legacy is something that "just happens" if you live long enough.

That's not true.

Legacy is crafted.
Legacy is planned.
Legacy is created.
Legacy is built piece by piece through decisions, discipline, vision, and consistency.

Legacy is shaped by:

- The habits you model
- The systems you create
- The people you lift
- The opportunities you build
- The businesses you scale
- The assets you accumulate
- The impact you make
- The lessons you teach
- The doors you open

And most importantly: Legacy comes from refusing to let your past repeat through the people you love.

Framework:

The Real Life XP Legacy System

This system has 5 components:

1. Personal Legacy (Who You Become)

This is the version of you your children, family, community, or followers will remember.

Ask yourself:

- Who am I becoming?
- What values do I live by?
- What habits define me?
- What example am I setting?
- What impact do I want to have as a human being?
- How will people describe me when I'm gone?

This shapes your identity legacy.

2. Business Legacy (What You Build)

Your business can become:

- An asset
- A system
- A vehicle
- A job creator
- A community resource
- A family foundation
- A generational opportunity

This is where you shift from entrepreneur to owner.

3. Financial Legacy (What You Leave)

This is about:

- Assets
- Investments
- Property
- Business equity
- Trusts
- Life insurance
- Family financial planning
- Wealth systems
- Ownership

This is how you change your family tree.

4. Community Legacy (Who You Impact)

This includes:

- Mentoring
- Teaching
- Coaching
- Giving back
- Donating
- Volunteering
- Creating programs

- Creating opportunities
- Supporting the next generation

Your journey becomes someone else's hope.

5. Generational Legacy (What Continues)

This is the final stage.

It includes:

- Estate planning
- Succession planning
- Next-gen leadership
- Systems that outlive you
- Businesses that run without you
- Wealth that continues to grow
- Impact that keeps touching lives

This is how you create permanence.

Coach JP Insight (Raw Truth):

Your family has suffered enough.

Your community has struggled enough.
The cycle ends with you.

You didn't go through those hard years for nothing.
You didn't survive trauma to pass down trauma.
You didn't escape old environments just to recreate them.
You didn't break the pattern just to let it rebuild itself.

You are the generational turning point.
You are the pattern breaker.
You are the one your future family will thank.
You are the one your community will point to.
You are the one who changes the direction of the story.

Legacy starts now.

Common Mistakes (XP Corrections)

Mistake 1: Living only for today

Correction:
Plan for the version of you 20 years from now.

Mistake 2: Thinking legacy requires millions

Correction:
Legacy starts with values, not dollars.

Mistake 3: Not documenting your business

Correction:
Documented systems create transferable businesses.

Mistake 4: Avoiding estate planning

Correction:
Protect your legacy on paper.

Mistake 5: Thinking your story isn't powerful

Correction:
Someone is waiting for the chapter you're hiding.

Real Life Application (Implementation Steps)

Step 1: Define Your Legacy Statement

Write one paragraph: "What do I want my life to mean?"

Step 2: Build Your Family Protection Plan

This includes:

- Life insurance
- Will
- Trust
- Beneficiaries
- Emergency plan

Step 3: Document Your Business Systems

Your business must be transferable and operable.

Step 4: Begin Long-Term Investing

Stocks, real estate, retirement accounts, business assets.

Step 5: Identify Your Impact Area

Decide where you want to give back and how.

Exercises + Worksheets

Exercise 1: Legacy Identity Worksheet

Write:

- How I want to be remembered
- What values matter to me
- What habits I want to model
- What standards I want to set

Exercise 2: Generational Wealth Starter Plan

List:

- Assets you currently have
- Assets you want to acquire
- Steps to begin building

Exercise 3: Impact Map

Write down:

- Who you want to help
- How you want to help them
- Why it matters to you

Exercise 4: Business Continuity Plan

If you took 6 months off, what needs to happen so your business still runs?

Reflection & Journal Prompts

- What does "legacy" mean to me personally?
- Who do I want to become for the next generation?
- What part of my story could change someone else's life?
- What do I want my children or community to inherit besides money?
- What do I want to leave behind that lasts longer than I do?

Closing Motivation

You are not just building a business, you're building a future.

You are not just serving clients, you're shaping generations.

You are not just making money, you're breaking cycles.

You are not just setting goals, you're setting foundations.

Legacy & Impact is the pillar that turns your effort into eternity.
It turns your struggle into strength.
It turns your pain into purpose.
It turns your business into a blessing.

You are writing a story that won't end when your life does, and that is the highest level of entrepreneurship.

Your legacy begins today. And the world will feel it long after you're gone.

CONCLUSION

THE REAL LIFE XP FRAMEWORK

Where Your Journey Becomes Your Power

Take a breath. Look at everything you just walked through: the pillars, the stories, the frameworks, the systems, the strategies. But more importantly

Look at yourself.

You're not the same entrepreneur who started Chapter 1.
You're not the same person who came into this book hoping for clarity.
You're not the same leader who used to operate in survival mode.
You've grown.
You've expanded.
You've matured.
You've awakened something inside you that was always there but needed structure, direction, and intention.

This book didn't give you anything new. It unlocked what was already in you.

Real Life XP was never about hype, motivation, or "get rich quick" energy. It was built for entrepreneurs like you, real people, with real experiences, facing real challenges.

You didn't build your life on easy.
You built it on grit.
On pressure.
On lessons learned the hard way.
On strength you didn't know you had.

On environments that didn't set you up.
On obstacles that didn't stop you.

And now? Now you're building differently.

You Aren't Just Building a Business.

You're Building Yourself. Let's bring the Seven Pillars back into your mind:

1. **Mindset & Motivation** - your internal engine
2. **Business Formation & Systems** - your structural foundation
3. **Process & Automation** - your operational freedom
4. **Credit & Capital** - your financial power
5. **Marketing & Branding** - your visibility and influence
6. **Leadership & Team Building** - your multiplication
7. **Legacy & Impact** - your eternal footprint

These aren't random concepts. These are the seven skills every entrepreneur must master to scale in the REAL world. Not the Instagram world. Not the theory world. Not the highlight-reel world. But the world you live in is the one that tests you, molds you, exposes you, and demands your best. Each pillar builds on the next. Each pillar transforms your capacity. Each pillar strengthens your foundation. Each pillar shapes you into the kind of entrepreneur who doesn't just survive… but LEADS.

Your Transformation = Your Trajectory

As you worked through these chapters, something happened: you began to shift. You began to think like a CEO, not a survivor. You began to build systems, not excuses. You began to choose structure, not chaos. You began to embrace leadership, not overwork. You began to move with intention, not reaction. You began to talk legacy, not just income. And once you shift like this, your business cannot stay the same. Your life cannot stay the same. Your future cannot stay the same. This is the beginning of your next level, not the end.

What You Build Now Will Shape Generations

- Maybe you didn't grow up with guidance.
- Maybe you didn't start with money.
- Maybe you didn't have mentors.
- Maybe you didn't have stability.
- Maybe you didn't have the support you deserved.
- Maybe you had to figure it all out the hard way.

But look at you now.

- ✓ You're building systems.
- ✓ You're developing discipline.
- ✓ You're creating structure.
- ✓ You're learning leadership.
- ✓ You're expanding capacity.
- ✓ You're elevating your mindset.
- ✓ You're building something REAL.
- ✓ Something sustainable.
- ✓ Something scalable.
- ✓ Something powerful.
- ✓ You are becoming the person you once needed.
- ✓ You are becoming the blueprint.
- ✓ You are becoming the standard.
- ✓ You are becoming the turning point in your family story.
- ✓ You are becoming the leader your community can trust.
- ✓ You are becoming the entrepreneur your younger self prayed for.

Legacy doesn't start when life ends; it starts when purpose begins. And your purpose has just activated.

The XP Promise

A Message from Coach JP:

I built this framework because I know what it feels like to start from nothing. I know what it feels like to feel unsupported, unseen, unheard, and unprepared. I know what it feels like to fight through systems that weren't built for us. I know what it feels like to struggle with mindset, = money, marketing, and motivation all at the same time. But I also know what it feels like to rise.

To build structure.
To create systems.
To break patterns.
To scale.
To lead.
To impact.
To transform.
To change your life from the inside out.

Real Life XP is the bridge between where you come from and where you're meant to go. This framework isn't just a book.

It's a roadmap.
It's a strategy.
It's a structure.
It's a mirror.
It's a shift.

And if you let it, it will become the accelerator that takes you further than you've ever been.

Your Next Step:

Move from Learning to Leadership

You've read.
You've grown.
You've reflected.
Now it's time to APPLY.

Because information without action is entertainment. And you weren't built for entertainment you were built for elevation.

Here's your next step:

Take each pillar and begin implementing one part of it every week. Small steps. Simple changes. Consistent execution. Before you realize it, you'll look up and see:

- Your business is structured.
- Your systems are working.
- Your income is increasing.
- Your leadership is growing.
- Your influence is spreading.
- Your impact is multiplying.
- Your legacy is forming.

The Seven Pillars are not a theory. They are a transformation. And now it's your turn to walk it out.

You Are the XP.

Your Life Is the Testimony.
Your Success Is the Impact.
Your Legacy Starts Now.

This is the end of the book but the beginning of the era where you lead your business with intention, structure, and power. You've unlocked your next level. Now go build it.

FINAL WORD FROM COACH JP

Your Next Level Starts When You Decide to Step into It

If you made it to this page, I want you to pause and acknowledge something powerful:

- You are not here by accident.
- You didn't stumble onto this book by chance.
- You didn't invest your time, energy, or attention into this journey for nothing.
- Something in you is ready.
- Something in you is shifting.
- Something in you is waking up.

As you've read through the Seven Pillars, you've felt the truth in them. You've seen yourself in them. You've seen your struggles, your strengths, your potential, and your future. You've been shown a framework but more importantly you've been shown your next level.

Now the question becomes:

What will you do with this? Because knowledge can inspire you but action will transform you.

Reading this book is step one. Implementing it is step two. But walking this journey with a coach, a community, and a proven system behind you? That's where exponential progress becomes real. That's where XP becomes your lifestyle not just your learning.

Why I Created the Real Life XP Six-Week Entrepreneur Acceleration Program

I built the Real Life XP Coaching Program for people like you entrepreneurs with real responsibilities, real pressure, real pasts, and real dreams.

It's for entrepreneurs who have:

- the drive but need structure
- the work ethic but need systems
- the ideas but need clarity
- the hustle but need strategy
- the potential but need accountability
- the discipline but need direction
- the passion but need a proven path

This six-week coaching program is the most powerful, focused, transformative business training experience I've ever created.

Where the book teaches you the framework the coaching program walks with you step-by-step as you build it. This isn't "information. This is implementation. You won't just read the Seven Pillars

You'll apply them.
You'll build them.
You'll install them.
You'll embody them.
You'll build systems.
You'll get structured.
You'll develop consistency.
You'll understand your numbers.
You'll fix your mindset.
You'll strengthen your foundation.
You'll create processes.
You'll automate your business.
You'll identify new revenue opportunities.
You'll build the confidence of a CEO who knows exactly what they're doing.

And you will not do this alone. You'll do it with:

- me
- my team
- your cohort
- weekly accountability
- live coaching
- real worksheets
- real structure
- real guidance
- real transformation

This is where the XP framework stops being a concept and becomes something that drives your business every single day.

A Personal Promise from Me to You

Before you close this book, I want you to hear this: I'm not here to sell you hype. I'm here to give you a structure that WORKS because I know what's on the other side of struggle when you finally get the right guidance.

I built Real Life XP for entrepreneurs like us. Entrepreneurs who weren't handed a blueprint. Entrepreneurs who didn't grow up with a safety net. Entrepreneurs who had to survive before they learned how to scale. Entrepreneurs who need something deeper than "motivation." Entrepreneurs who need real structure, real accountability, and real systems. You deserve that support. You deserve that clarity. You deserve that elevation. And you deserve access to the coaching that took me years to build. You don't have to do this alone anymore. You don't have to guess anymore. You don't have to carry your business quietly in your head anymore. Let me help you build the business that matches your potential.

YOUR NEXT STEP

Join the Real Life XP Six-Week Coaching Program

If you're ready to:

- get structured

- build systems
- create automation
- clarify your brand
- strengthen your mindset
- develop consistency
- build confidence
- eliminate chaos
- grow your revenue
- scale with strategy
- accelerate your progress
- and experience exponential progress (XP)

then it's time.

Go to: www.RealLifeXP.com.
Complete the application form.
Book your onboarding call.
Start your transformation.

This is your moment.

Not tomorrow.
Not next month.
Not "when things slow down."
Not "when life gets easier."
Not "when I feel ready."

You become ready by deciding. You transform by acting. You elevate by investing in yourself, your business, and your future. I'm ready to coach you. My team is ready to support you. Your next level is waiting for you. All you have to do is take the step. **www.RealLifeXP.com** Complete the form. Start the journey. Build the life and business you were meant to live.

See you inside.

— **Coach JP**

BOOK 2

THE SEVEN STAGES OF SCALING™

The Real Life OS for Predictable, Sustainable Growth

Alvin C. Hill IV, MBA (Coach JP)

TABLE OF CONTENTS

INTRODUCTION

WHY MOST ENTREPRENEURS NEVER SCALE AND

How This Book Gives You the Roadmap They Never Had

There comes a point in every entrepreneur's journey where you look around and realize something uncomfortable:

You're working too hard for the amount of progress you're making.

You're dedicated.
You're grinding.
You're committed.
You're pushing.
You're giving everything you've got.

But the results? They don't match the effort. And you start wondering:

- What am I missing?
- Why does success feel inconsistent?
- Why do I grow, then stall, then grow, then stall again?
- Why does it feel like every win comes with another fire to put out?
- Why isn't my business scaling the way I want it to?

It's not because you're not talented.
It's not because you're not disciplined.
It's not because you're not smart enough.
It's not because entrepreneurship isn't for you.

It's because **nobody ever showed you the stages of scaling in order.**

You were told to "grind."

But not how to grow.

You were told to "market more."

But not how to stabilize your systems.

You were told to "raise your prices."

But not when you're structurally ready.

You were told to "automate."

But not what to automate first.

You were told to "build a team."

But not when you can afford one or how to lead one.

In other words:

You were given pieces but never the full path. That's where this book comes in.

The Real Life OS:

A Scaling Framework Built for Real Entrepreneurs with Real Challenges.

The Seven Stages of Scaling™ were not created in a classroom.
They weren't copied from another business book.
They weren't pulled from a theory.

Like Real Life XP, this framework was **built in the trenches**:

- While running real businesses
- While mentoring minority entrepreneurs
- While watching people succeed and fail
- While studying the patterns of growth and collapse
- While testing strategies under real-life pressure
- While helping entrepreneurs who didn't start with advantages

Through observation, coaching, experience, and pattern recognition, I realized something profound:

Entrepreneurs don't fail because they're unqualified, they fail because they move out of order.

They skip steps.
They jump ahead.
They build prematurely.
They try to scale without stabilizing.
They try to expand without the foundation.
They try to automate before they have clarity.
They try to grow before the business is even ready.

Scaling is not magic.
Scaling is not "try harder."
Scaling is not "just hire."
Scaling is not "run more ads."
Scaling is a SEQUENCE.

A predictable, proven, step-by-step progression that every successful business travels through from idea to empire. Once you understand the sequence, everything becomes clear.

Linear Growth vs. Exponential Progress (XP)

Why These Stages Unlock the Fastest Version of You

Book 1: taught you the Seven Pillars - the skills and competencies that make you strong internally and structurally.

Book 2: teaches you the **path** - the order of operations.

This is where you stop growing linearly and start scaling exponentially.

Linear growth is:

- slow
- inconsistent

- exhausting
- dependent on you doing everything manually

Exponential Progress (XP) is:

- ✓ strategic
- ✓ predictable
- ✓ structured
- ✓ automated
- ✓ team-supported
- ✓ system-driven

Once you follow the Seven Stages, your business grows:

- faster
- smoother
- stronger
- with less emotional chaos
- and with more confidence

XP momentum is not hype, it's math. Each stage multiplies the one before it. That's why this book is called **The Real Life OS** because it upgrades your internal software as a CEO and your external systems as a company.

Who This Book Is For

This book is designed specifically for:

Minority entrepreneurs

who need a roadmap that makes sense in real life, not in theory?

Service-based business owners

building from organic growth into predictable acquisition.

Entrepreneurs who have outgrown hustle

and need structure, strategy, and sustainable scaling.

Business owners who feel stuck at the same revenue level

and don't know what's missing.

Leaders who are ready to grow…

but can't afford to grow the wrong way.

Anyone who wants to build something stable, scalable, and legacy-focused

instead of a stressful, inconsistent grind.

If you want to grow smarter, not harder…
If you want to scale without burnout…
If you want to turn chaos into clarity…
If you want to turn effort into results…

This book is for you.

How This Book Works

Each stage is its own complete chapter.

You will find:

- A powerful opening story
- Deep teaching
- A Real Life XP Principle
- A scaling framework
- Common mistakes
- Implementation steps
- Worksheets & exercises
- Reflection prompts
- "Coach JP Insight" sections
- Motivational closing paragraphs

Each chapter builds on the stage before it.

- Do NOT skip ahead.
- Do NOT combine stages.
- Do NOT guess.
- ✓ Follow the order.
- ✓ Follow the sequence.
- ✓ Follow the system.

Scaling is not random; it's a rhythm. And by the time you finish this book, you won't just understand scaling. You'll be READY for it.

CHAPTER 1

STAGE ONE ENERGIZE (IDEA → ACTION)

The Momentum Stage: Where Vision Becomes Movement

Every business, no matter how big, successful, or established, starts in the exact same place:

- A **spark**.
- A problem you see.
- A solution you believe in.
- A vision you can't let go of.
- A feeling that says, "There's something I'm supposed to build."

But for most entrepreneurs, the spark never becomes a fire.

Not because the idea wasn't good.
Not because the timing wasn't right.
Not because they didn't want it bad enough.

But because they never entered the first stage of scaling:

ENERGIZE - the stage where ideas turn into action, and action turns into identity.

This is the stage that separates dreamers from doers. This is where your vision stops being a thought and becomes the first step toward your future. Energize is not about perfection.

It's about **activation**. It's the stage where you learn to move. Where you learn to believe. Where you build the internal momentum you will need for the journey ahead.

Everything begins here.

Opening Story:

The Night I Decided I Was Done Waiting on "The Right Time"

I remember the night I made the decision.

Not the decision to "try."
Not the decision to "plan."
Not the decision to "think about it."

The decision to **start**.

To move.
To act.
To build something real, even if I didn't know all the answers.

Up until that night, I was like everyone else:

- waiting for more money
- waiting for more time
- waiting for more confidence
- waiting for more clarity
- waiting for the perfect moment

But here's the truth:

- **There is no perfect moment.**
- **There is no moment without fear.**
- **There is no moment without uncertainty.**
- **There is only the moment you DECIDE.**

I had bought courses, watched YouTube, followed gurus, listened to podcasts. but I wasn't progressing. I was consuming not creating. And one night I realized the truth:

Information wasn't my problem. Inaction was.

That night, I made a promise to myself: "I will not let another year go by thinking about the business I should've built." That was my Energize moment.
And when you have yours?
Everything changes.

Big Idea of Stage One:

Action Creates Clarity, Not the Other Way Around

Most entrepreneurs get stuck in *planning mode.*

They want to:

- research
- study
- organize
- prepare
- perfect

BEFORE they take action. But that mindset kills businesses before they start.

You don't gain confidence first.
You don't gain clarity first.
You don't gain certainty first.

You gain those things THROUGH ACTION. Entrepreneurs who scale learn this quickly:

You don't learn and then act.

You act and then learn. This is why Stage One is called **Energize**.

Because this stage is all about building your momentum:

- mentally
- emotionally
- creatively
- operationally
- energetically

Without momentum, the rest of the journey doesn't matter.

Real Life XP Principle #1:

Movement Before Mastery

You don't need mastery to move. But you DO need movement to reach mastery. The biggest mistake entrepreneurs make is believing, "I need to know everything before I begin." No, you need to begin. Because movement teaches you what matters.

Movement shows you the path.
Movement gives you feedback.
Movement reveals the next step.
Movement builds belief.

Action is the antidote to fear.
Action is the accelerant of clarity.
Action is the foundation of success.

The Real Life XP Energize Framework (A → C → E)

Your first stage has three components:

A - Awareness

Become aware of:

- the problem you solve
- the people who need it
- the value you bring
- the skills you already have
- the gaps you need to fill
- the opportunities around you

Clarity begins with awareness.

C - Commitment

You must commit before you're confident.

This commitment includes:

- deciding to start
- setting a date
- choosing your first offer
- choosing your target audience
- choosing your first 3 steps
- creating a weekly business rhythm

Commitment is where ideas become real.

E - Execution

This is where most people fail and where XP entrepreneurs thrive.

Execution at this stage is simple:

- Sell the idea before you build it
- Get feedback fast
- Create before you consume
- Make the first dollar
- Build the first process
- Take action DAILY

Execution gives you momentum, and momentum gives you belief.

Coach JP Insight (Raw Truth):

If you don't start now, you won't start later. Your "later" is just fear wearing a mask. I've coached hundreds of entrepreneurs. And I can tell you EXACTLY who scales and who stalls. The ones who scale take messy action. The ones who stall take perfect notes.

Every excuse: "I'm not ready," "I need more time," "I need more money," "I need more clarity," is just fear dressed up as logic.

You don't need more of anything. You need more movement. Start. And everything changes. Every. Single. Time.

Common Mistakes in Stage One (XP Corrections)

Mistake 1: Overplanning

Correction:
Set a 14-day deadline and START.

Mistake 2: Waiting for confidence

Correction:
Confidence is built through doing.

Mistake 3: Starting too big

Correction:
Start with a simple, high-value offer.

Mistake 4: Consuming more than creating

Correction:
For every hour you learn, take an hour of ACTION.

Mistake 5: Thinking you need everything perfect

Correction:
Progress beats perfection every time.

Real Life Application (Implementation Steps)

Here's how you activate Stage One this week:

Step 1 - Write Your Starter Statement

> "What problem do I solve and for whom?"

Step 2 - Create Your First Offer

One problem → one promise → one price.

Step 3 - Build Your Action Rhythm

3–5 non-negotiable actions per week.

Step 4 - Get Your First Yes

Sell BEFORE you build. Proof comes from people paying, not people clapping.

Step 5 - Start Your Momentum Tracker

Track daily effort, not outcomes.

Worksheets & Exercises

Exercise 1: The 48-Hour Activation Plan

List 5 actions you can take in the next 48 hours to create momentum.

Exercise 2: Fear → Fuel Conversion

Write your biggest fear.
Then write the opposite action you must take.

Exercise 3: Starter Offer Builder

Fill in:

- I help ______
- solve ______
- by ______
- so they can ______

Exercise 4: Energize Journal Prompts

- What have I been delaying — and why?
- What would I do if I trusted myself more?
- What can I start TODAY that moves me forward?

Closing Motivation

You are stepping into a new identity right now, not someday, not later. Right. Now. Stage One is not about building the entire business. It's about sparking the energy that drives everything else. Your dream doesn't need permission. It needs a push. And this is that push. You don't get clarity by waiting. You get clarity by **moving.** You don't become unstoppable by thinking. You become unstoppable by **beginning.** Stage One is the stage of activation, alignment, and acceleration. And once you create momentum… the next six stages become inevitable.

CHAPTER 2

STAGE TWO - MONETIZE ($0 → $10K/MO)

The Validation Stage: Prove People Will Pay You

Stage One (Energize) is about moving from idea to action. Stage Two (Monetize) is about turning that action into **income**. This is the stage where you answer one of the most important questions in entrepreneurship: **"Will people actually pay me for this?"**

Not "Do people like it?"
Not "Do people support it?"
Not "Do people say I should start a business?"
Not "Do people comment fire emojis when I post about it?"

But WILL. THEY. PAY.

This is the point where you stop guessing and start validating. Where your dream becomes a real offer. Where your purpose becomes profitable. Where your confidence begins to take shape because now the market is responding. $0 to $10K/month is not about branding. Not about logos. Not about funnels. Not about complicated marketing. It's about creating an irresistible solution and getting people to say YES. If you do Stage Two right, the entire rest of the scaling journey becomes easier. If you skip Stage Two or do it halfway, you will struggle at every stage beyond this one. Let's do it the right way.

Opening Story:

The First Time I Realized People Would Pay Me for What I Knew

When I first started consulting and coaching, I had one fear: "What if nobody pays me?"

I knew I had value.
I knew I had experience.
I knew I had a story.
I knew I had insight.
I knew I could help people make progress.

But knowing YOURSELF is not the same as a MARKET knowing you. So I did something most entrepreneurs never do: I made the offer BEFORE I felt ready. And the craziest thing happened Someone said yes. That "yes" changed everything. Not because of the money but because of the belief it created. That first yes confirmed:

- my offer was needed
- my skills were valuable
- my story mattered
- my perspective was useful
- my approach was different
- my business could work

It was the validation that donors, followers, likes, and "supportive comments" could never give me.

The market spoke, and the market said GO.

That was my Stage Two moment. And now it's your turn.

Big Idea of Stage Two:

You Don't Have a Business Until Money Moves

Most people never reach this stage because they get stuck:

- creating content
- planning

- waiting
- worrying
- overthinking
- building websites
- designing logos
- tweaking branding
- "perfecting" their offer

But hear this clearly:

If nobody has paid you,

you don't have a business, you have a project. The transition from project to business happens when someone gives you money in exchange for your solution. That's Stage Two.

This is where you:

- test your idea
- refine your offer
- get feedback
- understand your audience
- create testimonials
- build confidence
- start momentum
- learn the market
- sharpen your sales
- build belief in yourself

This stage is not about scale. It's about **validation**.

Real Life XP Principle #2:

Money Is the Best Feedback

In the real world, people don't spend money on "nice ideas."

They spend money on:

- solutions

- relief
- transformation
- time-saving
- problem-solving
- life-changing
- results

When someone pays you, it tells you: "This problem is important. This solution is valuable. Keep going." When someone doesn't pay, it tells you: "The offer needs work. The messaging needs clarity. The price needs positioning. The audience needs refining." Either way, you WIN because money gives you honest feedback. Likes don't. Comments don't. Followers don't. Money is the truth.

The Real Life XP Monetize Framework (S.O.L.D.)

To go from $0 → $10K/mo, focus on four elements:

S - Solve One Painful Problem

Not ten.
Not five.
One.

Your whole business should start with ONE transformational solution.

People pay fastest for relief from pain.

Examples:

- "I help moms get energy back."
- "I help entrepreneurs build business credit."
- "I help handymen organize operations."
- "I help women lose 20 lbs in 90 days."
- "I help small businesses get more leads."

The more specific the problem…
the easier the sale.

O - Offer a Clear, Compelling Promise

Your offer must answer:

- What problem do you solve?
- What result do you deliver?
- How fast will they see progress?
- Why is your method different?
- What transformation can they expect?

People don't buy services.
People buy outcomes.

L - Leverage Conversations (Not Complicated Funnels)

Early-stage sales come from:

- DMs
- voice notes
- simple calls
- referrals
- inbox conversations
- short videos
- community networks
- You don't need ads yet.
- You don't need funnels yet.
- You don't need automation yet.

You need CONVERSATIONS.

Your first $10K will come from talking to people not tech.

D - Deliver a High-Value Experience

Your first clients become:

- your testimonials
- your case studies
- your referrals
- your early advocates
- your learning laboratory

Give them transformation. Give them results. Give them value that feels "too good for the price." This is where your brand begins to build power.

Coach JP Insight (Raw Truth):

You don't need more followers.

You need more offers. People say: "I need more followers before I can sell." But let me tell you this: You can make $10K/month with 300 followers if your offer is strong and your message is clear. You can have 10,000 followers and still be broke if you never sell anything. Visibility helps. But **offers make money**.

In Stage Two, your job is not to be famous. Your job is to be **profitable**.

Common Mistakes in Stage Two (XP Corrections)

Mistake 1: Creating too many offers

Correction:
One problem → one offer → one audience.

Mistake 2: Underpricing

Correction:
Price based on VALUE, not insecurity.

Mistake 3: Avoiding sales conversations

Correction:
Selling is serving.

Mistake 4: Building funnels too early

Correction:
Master organic conversations first.

Mistake 5: Thinking money will come "when you're ready"

Correction:
Make the offer NOW. Refine later.

Real Life Application (Implementation Steps)

Step 1: Define the ONE problem you solve

The more painful the problem, the easier the sale.

Step 2: Create your MVP offer (Minimum Viable Product)

1 problem
1 promise
1 price
1 process

Step 3: Send 20 "Value Starter" Messages

Example:
"Hey, I'm putting together a new program that helps ______. Would you be open to hearing more?"

Step 4: Take 5 sales calls this week

Conversations = Cash.

Step 5: Deliver transformation

Your early clients become the seeds of your future scale.

Worksheets & Exercises

Exercise 1: Power Problem Audit

List 3 problems you can solve.
Circle the one with the most pain.

Exercise 2: Offer Builder Template

I help ______
solve ______
so they can ______
in ______ timeframe
through ______ method.

Exercise 3: Monetize Action Map

Write your first 10 people to message.
Send the messages TODAY.

Exercise 4: Fearless Sales Journal

- What scares me about selling?
- What belief is holding me back?
- What would the confident version of me say?

Closing Motivation

This stage changes everything.

This is the stage where you PROVE to yourself and the world:

- I can make money.
- I can help people.
- I can sell.
- I can deliver.
- I can build something real.
- I can turn my idea into income.

Monetize is not about the money.
It's about the movement.
It's about proving that your business has legs.
It's about building belief so strong
it carries you into Stage Three with confidence and clarity.

Your clients are waiting.
Your moment is here.
Your business begins now.

CHAPTER 3

STAGE THREE — STABILIZE ($10K → $30K/MO)

The Consistency Stage: Build Predictable Revenue & Stop the Chaos

Stage Two (Monetize) proves your offer works. But Stage Three (Stabilize) proves your business works.

This is the stage where you shift from:

- inconsistent → reliable
- emotional → structured
- chaotic → controlled
- reactive → intentional
- guessing → tracking
- hustling → operating

Stage Two produces your first income. Stage Three produces your first predictable income. This is where things become REAL. You're no longer asking, "Can I make money?" Now you're asking, "Can I make money consistently?" If Stage Two is about validation, Stage Three is about FOUNDATION. Because you cannot scale chaos. You cannot automate inconsistency. You cannot delegate confusion. You cannot stabilize what you haven't structured.

Stage Three is the backbone of the entire scaling journey.

Opening Story:

The Month I Realized My Income Was High, but My Business Was Low

I'll never forget the month I made great money but still felt broke. Not because of the revenue. But because of the **rhythm**. One week I had clients. Next week I didn't. One day I was overwhelmed with calls. Next day I had nothing on the calendar. One month looked amazing. The next month looked scary. And then it hit me: **I didn't have a business problem. I had a consistency problem.**

I wasn't struggling with sales, I was struggling with structure.

My income wasn't predictable because my systems weren't predictable. I felt overworked and under-supported because nothing in my business was stable. I didn't need more clients, I needed more systems. I didn't need more hustle I needed more organization. I didn't need to grind harder, I needed to build better.

Stage Three is where I learned:

- **Success is not built on effort.**
- **Success is built on structure.**

And that changed everything.

Big Idea of Stage Three:

You Don't Have a Business Until You Have a SYSTEM That Produces Consistent Revenue at $10K/month, you DO NOT need:

- a big team
- ads
- complicated funnels
- major software
- advanced automation
- expensive branding

What you need is:

A repeatable client acquisition system that works EVEN when you're tired, busy, or not at 100%. In other words, A business that keeps going instead of one that falls apart every time life gets real. And for minority entrepreneurs, this stage is especially important.

Because life WILL get real:

- kids
- work
- family
- stress
- unexpected setbacks
- responsibilities
- mental health
- financial pressure

You need a business that survives those moments, not collapses during them.

That's what Stage Three creates.

Real Life XP Principle #3:

Stability Creates Scalability

You CANNOT amplify something that is unstable.

If your revenue is unstable, your growth will be unstable.
If your leads are unstable, your income will be unstable.
If your processes are unstable, your delivery will be unstable.

Stability isn't sexy.
It's not flashy.
It doesn't go viral.

But stability is the quiet force that makes scaling possible.

Stage Three is where you learn:

Consistency beats intensity.
Systems beat stress.
Structure beats hustle.

The Real Life XP "Stability Engine" (T.L.C.)

There are three core components you MUST build at this stage:

T - Traffic Rhythm (Leads Coming In Consistently)

You need **a simple, repeatable lead-generation routine**.

Examples:

- 3–5 posts per week
- daily engagement
- weekly value email
- partnerships
- referrals
- outreach rhythm
- one weekly promotional piece

No need for ads yet.
No need for complex funnels.

Just simple, predictable activity.

L - Lead Nurture System (Turning Attention into Appointments)

Most entrepreneurs sell too soon or not at all.

You need:

- follow-up scripts
- DM frameworks
- weekly nurture content
- a lead tracker

- weekly reporting
- a simple CRM or spreadsheet

People don't buy instantly, they buy when they feel ready. Nurture gets them ready.

C - Conversion Routine (A Consistent Way to Close Sales)

You need a simple offer → conversation → close system.

This includes:

- a clear sales script
- an onboarding process
- closing questions
- pricing structure
- payment system
- call-to-action clarity

Your sales process doesn't need to be perfect.
It needs to be consistent.

Coach JP Insight (Raw Truth):

You're not overwhelmed because you're growing.

You're overwhelmed because you have no structure. Let me be blunt:

- You're tired because you're managing chaos.
- You're inconsistent because your systems are inconsistent.
- You're stressed because your business lives in your HEAD instead of on PAPER.
- This is why you feel like you're always starting over.
- This is why every month feels like a gamble.
- This is why progress feels fragile.
- This is why your confidence keeps rising and falling.

You don't need more motivation. You need more management. Stabilize your systems and your stress disappears.

Common Mistakes in Stage Three (XP Corrections)

Mistake 1: Free-styling everything

Correction:
Document daily & weekly rhythms.

Mistake 2: Relying on "feeling motivated"

Correction:
Structure creates consistency even when emotions shift.

Mistake 3: No lead nurture system

Correction:
Follow-up = fortune.

Mistake 4: Changing offers too quickly

Correction:
Your offer needs time to mature.

Mistake 5: Scaling too early

Correction:
Fix inconsistencies BEFORE automating or hiring.

Real Life Application (Implementation Steps)

Step 1: Create a Weekly Marketing Rhythm

Example:

- 3 content pieces
- 1 CTA post
- 1 value email
- 20 minutes of daily engagement

Step 2: Build a Lead Tracker

Track:

- name
- contact method
- date added
- follow-up
- next action
- stage in pipeline

Step 3: Standardize Your Sales Process

Create a repeatable script + onboarding workflow.

Step 4: Set Weekly KPIs

Examples:

- leads generated
- appointments booked
- sales calls taken
- revenue collected
- retention rate

Step 5: Evaluate Monthly Stability

Ask:

- Was my revenue predictable?
- Did I follow the rhythm?
- Did my system break?
- Where did inconsistency show up?

Worksheets & Exercises

Exercise 1: Stability Scorecard

Rate yourself (1–10) on:

- lead generation
- sales rhythm

- nurture pipeline
- content consistency
- sales process
- offer consistency
- emotional discipline

Exercise 2: Chaos → Clarity Map

Write down everything chaotic. Rewrite each item as a system.

Exercise 3: Weekly Rhythm Builder

Plan your weekly routine hour-by-hour.

Exercise 4: Stabilize Journal Prompts

- What areas of my business feel unpredictable?
- What does a stable version of me look like?
- What ONE habit could change my consistency forever?

Closing Motivation

This stage is not glamorous. It's not shiny.
It's not "viral." But it is POWERFUL.

Because Stabilize is the stage that:

- protects your peace
- strengthens your foundation
- balances your emotions
- creates consistency
- builds confidence
- improves your delivery
- increases retention
- makes income predictable

Stability is strength.

Stability is leadership.
Stability is maturity.
Stability is freedom.

And once your business becomes stable. You are finally ready for Stage Four where we take your proven offer and turn it into something scalable.

CHAPTER 4

STAGE FOUR - PRODUCTIZE ($30K → $100K/MO)

The Multiplication Stage: Turn Your Expertise Into a Scalable Asset

If Stage Three is about stability, Stage Four is about scalability. This is the moment when your business stops depending on your time, your hands, your calls, your presence, and your personality to grow and starts depending on systems, structure, and assets. In Stage Two, you learned to monetize. In Stage Three, you learned to stabilize. But in Stage Four? You learn to multiply. This stage is MASSIVE.

It is the bridge between:

- being booked
- and being a business
- being overwhelmed
- and being organized
- doing everything manually
- and creating leveraged products that scale without your constant effort

This is where you transform from **service provider → solution owner.** And from **hustler → architect.** Welcome to PRODUCTIZE, the stage that changes your business forever.

Opening Story:

The Moment I Realized I Was the Bottleneck

There was a period in my business where everything was going great and everything was going wrong at the same time.

I had clients.
I had demand.
I had results.
I had revenue coming in.

But deep down, I knew something wasn't right. Because every single thing depended on ME.

Every sale
Every session
Every question
Every deliverable
Every breakdown
Every fix
Every task
Every fire
Every follow-up

And it hit me:

I wasn't scaling my business. I was drowning in it.

My success had outgrown my structure.
My growth had outgrown my systems.
My demand had outgrown my capacity.

And then I realized the truth:

If my business cannot grow without me, then my business is NOT a business, it's just a job I built for myself.

Productizing my knowledge and systems changed everything. It turned my workload into workflows. It turned my expertise into assets. It turned my signature method into products that work WITHOUT me. And it will do the same for you.

Big Idea of Stage Four:

Your Business Must Shift from "Me" to "Model."

In Stage Four, your question becomes: "How do I take what I do and turn it into something that doesn't require ME to deliver every time?" This is where most entrepreneurs fail because they never make the transition from:

- service → system
- manual → repeatable
- 1:1 → 1: many
- custom work → standardized experience
- you doing everything → your method doing everything

This is the stage where you start creating:

- programs
- frameworks
- curriculum
- digital products
- onboarding systems
- delivery systems
- membership communities
- templates
- toolkits
- operations manuals

In short: **You turn your expertise into something scalable.**

Real Life XP Principle #4:

If your business depends on you, it can't scale.

If it depends on your system, it becomes unstoppable.

You don't scale by working harder.
You scale by creating things that work without you.

Your system becomes your salesperson.
Your curriculum becomes your coach.
Your process becomes your product.
Your framework becomes your foundation.

This is how real companies grow.

The Real Life XP Productize Framework (A.S.S.E.T.S.)

This is how you turn your expertise into a scalable business model:

A - Audit Your Delivery

Write down every step of:

- how you onboard clients
- how you deliver results
- how you solve problems
- how you communicate
- how you support clients

This gives you clarity on what to automate or standardize.

S - Standardize Your Method

Turn your process into:

- steps
- phases
- modules
- pillars

- frameworks

People don't buy "what you do." They buy **your method**.

S - Systematize Your Client Journey

Create a consistent path for clients:

- onboarding
- delivery
- communication
- fulfillment
- success tracking

This creates efficiency and consistency.

E - Extract Your Intellectual Property

This includes:

- templates
- scripts
- checklists
- worksheets
- email sequences
- SOPs
- curriculum

THIS is the gold inside your business.

T - Transform It Into a Product

Create:

- group coaching programs
- courses
- memberships
- hybrid programs
- digital products
- self-paced modules

Your product becomes your leverage.

S - Scale with Support

Now that you have systems, you can:

- hire a VA
- delegate delivery
- bring in coaches
- outsource admin
- expand marketing
- run ads
- increase volume

This is where real growth begins.

Coach JP Insight (Raw Truth):

Your business can't expand because YOU are in the way.

You are the bottleneck AND the breakthrough. This isn't judgment, it's awareness. If everything depends on you, you will ALWAYS hit capacity.

You will ALWAYS feel overwhelmed.
You will ALWAYS lack time.
You will ALWAYS limit growth.
You will ALWAYS feel stuck.

This stage forces you to:

- let go
- trust systems
- trust structure
- trust people
- trust your framework
- trust your process
- trust that you built something worthy of duplication

This is the stage where you learn to be a LEADER and not just a doer.

Common Mistakes in Stage Four (XP Corrections)

Mistake 1: Trying to scale too early

Correction:
Stabilize FIRST, productize SECOND.

Mistake 2: Creating products before systems

Correction:
Your method must be clear before you package it.

Mistake 3: Thinking your value disappears when your hands aren't on everything

Correction:
Your VALUE is in your METHOD, not your presence.

Mistake 4: Overcomplicating the product

Correction:
Simple → Scalable.

Mistake 5: Not documenting anything

Correction:
If it's not written, it can't be repeated.

Real Life Application (Implementation Steps)

Step 1: Document Your Signature Process

What are the steps you ALWAYS take to deliver transformation?

Step 2: Build Your First Productized Offer

Examples:

- A 6-week program
- A curriculum

- A course
- A membership

Step 3: Create Delivery Assets

- worksheets
- templates
- videos
- toolkits
- onboarding sequences

Step 4: Test Your Product with a Small Group

Your beta clients will give you feedback.

Step 5: Build Your Delivery Team

Hire:

- a VA
- a community manager
- an assistant coach
- a fulfillment specialist

but only AFTER your system is built.

Worksheets & Exercises

Exercise 1: Delivery Audit Map

Write every step of your client journey from "hello" to "results."

Exercise 2: Method Builder Worksheet

Outline your method into 3–7 phases.

Exercise 3: Product Idea Generator

List 3 ways to turn your method into scalable offers.

Exercise 4: Productize Journal Prompts

- What parts of my business MUST stop depending on me?
- What knowledge or process do I repeat over and over?
- What could become a template, module, or asset?

Closing Motivation

Stage Four is where everything changes.

This is the stage that frees your time.
This is the stage that multiplies your income.
This is the stage that increases your capacity.
This is the stage that builds a REAL company.
This is the stage that creates future wealth.
This is the stage that prepares you for SCALE.

Once you productize, your business stops growing "line by line" and starts growing layer by layer. You are not just building a business. You are building a MACHINE. And now that your system exists, you are finally ready for Stage Five, where the world begins to see you as an authority.

CHAPTER 5

STAGE FIVE — AMPLIFY ($100K → $300K/MO)

The Authority Stage: Turn Your Brand Into a Magnet & Multiply Your Reach

Stage Four gave you systems.
Stage Five gives you **scale**.

This is the stage where your brand stops whispering
and starts ROARING.

Where people don't "discover" you they seek you out.

Where your message becomes movement.
Where your authority becomes undeniable.
Where your marketing becomes magnetic.

In Stage Two, you learned how to sell.
In Stage Three, you learned how to stabilize.
In Stage Four, you learned how to productize.

But in Stage Five?

You learn how to **amplify** your voice
and expand your impact.

This is where the world starts paying attention.

Opening Story:

The Day I Realized My Brand Was Too Quiet for the Level of Success I Wanted

There was a time in my journey where everything was built, but nothing was loud.

My offer was good.
My systems were solid.
My delivery was consistent.
My clients were getting results.

But something was missing:

Visibility.

I wasn't showing up like the leader I knew I was.
I wasn't speaking boldly about my expertise.
I wasn't sharing the depth of my story.
I wasn't communicating my message clearly enough.
I wasn't strategic with my content.
I wasn't nurturing my audience.
I wasn't amplifying my brand.
I was hiding behind "humble."
I was hiding behind "private."
I was hiding behind "low-key."
I was hiding behind "I'll post when I feel like it."

But businesses don't scale in silence. Your authority is only as strong as your visibility. Your expertise is only as powerful as your communication. Your brand is only as magnetic as your consistency. And that day, I made a decision:

I refused to be invisible to people I was called to impact.

I stepped into my power.
I spoke louder.
I showed up daily.
I shared more boldly.

I told my story.
I taught from my heart.
I branded myself with intention.
I elevated my presence.

And the business followed. That's what Stage Five is about.

Big Idea of Stage Five:

You Cannot Scale Quietly.

For your business to grow exponentially, your brand must grow exponentially.

People must SEE you.
People must HEAR you.
People must FEEL you.
People must KNOW you.

This is the stage where you shift from:

- inconsistent → omnipresent
- unclear → undeniable
- passive → powerful
- quiet → magnetic
- invisible → influential

Stage Five is not about being "famous." It's about being found.

It's not about being a celebrity. It's about being a solution people recognize.

Amplify is not about ego it's about impact.

Real Life XP Principle #5:

Your voice is your vehicle.

Your brand is your bridge.
Your message is your magnet.
People don't follow products.

They follow people.
People don't engage with companies.
They engage with leaders.
People don't trust logos.
They trust identities.
Your authority is the ultimate amplifier.
Your brand is the ultimate shortcut.
Your message is the ultimate differentiator.

This is the stage where you build:

- credibility
- authority
- trust
- visibility
- resonance
- influence

Once people SEE you as a leader, they BUY from you as a leader.

The Real Life XP Amplify Framework (V.O.I.C.E.)

To amplify your business, you must amplify your **VOICE**:

V - Visibility Strategy

Where will you show up?

Choose 2 main platforms to dominate:

- TikTok
- Instagram
- Facebook
- YouTube
- LinkedIn
- Podcasts
- Events
- Webinars

Consistency here is EVERYTHING.

O - Omnipresent Content

You need content that works even when you're not.

Your content pillars should be:

- Value
- Story
- Proof
- Authority
- Call-to-action

Your content should answer:

- What do I believe?
- What do I teach?
- What do I stand for?
- What do I solve?
- Why am I the best?

Content makes noise.
Messages make movements.

I - Influence Marketing

This is where you expand your reach through:

- collaborations
- interviews
- joint ventures
- partnerships
- guest appearances
- community involvement

Your network becomes your amplifier.

C - Credibility Building

You need undeniable proof of your impact:

- testimonials
- transformations
- screenshots

- video reviews
- case studies
- milestone wins
- student highlights

People buy from those who deliver RESULTS.

E - Engagement Ecosystem

This is how you nurture your audience:

- email newsletters
- DMs
- live streams
- Q&A sessions
- free trainings
- community groups

People buy from those who communicate consistently.

Coach JP Insight (Raw Truth):

Your business isn't slow because your offer is weak.

It's slow because your presence is weak.
You're not lacking talent - you're lacking visibility.
You're not lacking value - you're lacking volume.
You're not lacking results - you're lacking reach.
You're not lacking clarity - you're lacking communication.

For many of us, especially minority entrepreneurs, we were taught to stay quiet, stay humble, stay low-key. But you can't change your life in silence. You can't lead people hiding in the shadows. You can't scale a brand nobody sees.

You deserve to be heard.
You deserve to be seen.
You deserve to take up space.

Amplify is where you step into that truth.

Common Mistakes in Stage Five (XP Corrections)

Mistake 1: Posting without strategy

Correction:
Follow your content pillars.

Mistake 2: Hiding your story

Correction:
Your story IS your authority.

Mistake 3: Inconsistency in brand identity

Correction:
Clear message. Clear visuals. Clear tone.

Mistake 4: Trying to amplify before productizing

Correction:
You must have delivery systems FIRST.

Mistake 5: Staying invisible out of fear

Correction:
Courage creates visibility; visibility creates opportunity.

Real Life Application (Implementation Steps)

Step 1: Choose Your Two Primary Platforms

Dominate them.

Step 2: Develop Your Content Pillars

Teach. Tell. Transform.

Step 3: Build Your Proof Portfolio

Collect every client win.

Step 4: Begin One Form of Weekly Long-Form Content

Examples:

- podcast
- YouTube
- weekly live
- weekly email

Step 5: Collaborate with One New Person Each Month

Expand your audience.

Worksheets & Exercises

Exercise 1: Brand Visibility Audit

Where am I showing up?
Where do I need to show up?

Exercise 2: Story Vault

List 10 stories you can share to build authority.

Exercise 3: Content Plan Builder

Plan one week of content for 2 platforms.

Exercise 4: Authority Prompts

- Why am I qualified?
- What makes my method different?
- What transformation do I create?

Closing Motivation

Stage Five is POWERFUL.

This is the stage where:

- ✓ people notice you
- ✓ clients find you
- ✓ partners reach out to you
- ✓ your momentum increases
- ✓ your income expands
- ✓ your impact multiplies

Amplify is the stage where your voice becomes a vehicle, and your brand becomes a bridge to the level of success you've been working toward. Once you amplify your authority, you are ready to handle more volume, more clients, more impact, and more growth. This leads us into Stage Six, where leadership and systems go to an entirely new level.

CHAPTER 6

STAGE SIX - ORGANIZE ($300K → $1M/YEAR)

The Infrastructure Stage: Build the Internal Machine That Allows You to Run a Real Company

Stage Five (Amplify) made your business loud.
Stage Six (Organize) makes your business LAST.

This is the stage where you stop operating like a high-performing hustler and start operating like a high-level company.

Your systems must mature.
Your team must expand.
Your operations must evolve.
Your leadership must strengthen.
Your infrastructure must hold heavier weight.

This is the stage where your internal world determines your external success.

You cannot scale powerfully if your backend is weak.
You cannot scale sustainably if your operations are sloppy.
You cannot scale confidently if your team is confused.
You cannot scale predictably if your data is untracked.
You cannot scale peacefully if everything depends on YOU.

Organize is the stage that transitions you from "running a business" to "leading an organization." This is where you build something that can actually HOLD the success you're creating.

Opening Story:

When Success Started Breaking My Business - Not Because It Was Too Small, But Because It Was Too Disorganized.

There was a season where my business was growing faster than ever.

- ✓ Great revenue.
- ✓ Great attention.
- ✓ Great demand.

But behind the scenes? It was falling apart.

- Clients slipping through cracks
- Tasks forgotten
- Team confused
- No documentation
- No workflow
- No metrics
- No accountability rhythm
- No clear leadership structure
- No onboarding system
- No SOPs
- No communication protocols

On the outside, everything looked like growth. On the inside, everything felt like chaos. And I realized something:

Success exposes disorganization.

The more your business grows, the more your weaknesses grow with it. And if you don't fix them, your growth will eventually collapse your business.

Stage Six forced me to face the truth:

It wasn't my revenue that was the problem; it was my lack of organization.

Once I fixed that?
My entire business transformed.

Systems carried the weight that stress used to carry.
Structure replaced chaos.

Clarity replaced confusion.
Team collaboration replaced burnout.
Operations replaced overwork.
Predictability replaced panic.

This stage will do the same for you.

Big Idea of Stage Six:

Your Business Must Become a Machine Before It Becomes a Movement

The difference between a business that scales and a business that struggles is simple:

Organization.

Here's what happens at this level:

- **Work increases exponentially**
- **Team expands**
- **Customers multiply**
- **Opportunities grow**
- **Volume gets heavier**
- **Marketing amplifies**
- **Delivery accelerates**

Without organization:

- mistakes multiply
- stress expands
- team fractures
- clients leave
- systems break
- success slows
- leadership collapses

Organization is not optional at this level. It's the only thing keeping your business from blowing up internally.

Real Life XP Principle #6:

Structure is the invisible power behind every successful company.

People admire the brand.
People admire the leader.
People admire the money.
People admire the impact.

But what they don't see is the structure holding all of it in place. Structure is the reason:

- Chick-fil-A operates flawlessly
- Apple delivers consistently
- Amazon ships reliably
- Starbucks scales continuously

Structure → Predictability
Predictability → Scalability
Scalability → Freedom

This stage is where your business becomes:

✓ organized
✓ efficient
✓ documented
✓ trackable
✓ optimized
✓ systemized

Once this happens, you unlock an entirely new level of growth.

The Real Life XP "Organize Engine" (P.E.O.P.L.E.)

At this stage, you build the six essential pillars of organizational structure:

P - Processes & SOPs

Your business must be documented.

- onboarding
- fulfillment
- sales
- customer service
- content creation
- reporting
- financial operations
- HR

If it's not written, it cannot be repeated.

E - Execution Systems

Here you build:

- project management workflow
- recurring task lists
- communication channels
- delivery timelines
- checklists
- automations
- calendars

This turns your business into a predictable machine.

O - Organizational Chart

Your team MUST have structure.

- roles
- responsibilities
- KPIs
- reporting lines

- accountability rhythms

Confusion kills companies. Clarity creates culture.

P - Performance Metrics & KPs

You need trackable numbers:

- leads
- close rate
- retention
- profitability
- fulfillment time
- customer satisfaction
- lifetime value
- marketing ROI
- team performance

What gets measured gets managed.
What gets managed gets mastered.

L - Leadership Systems

This includes:

- team meetings
- weekly check-ins
- scorecards
- coaching conversations
- performance reviews
- leadership communication

Your team is only as strong as your leadership rhythm.

E - Efficiency Tools

This is where you strategically integrate:

- CRMs
- automation tools
- AI systems

- communication platforms
- project management software

Tools don't fix disorganization; they amplify it. So you add tools AFTER your processes are defined.

Coach JP Insight (Raw Truth):

You're not failing - your business is unorganized.

Too many entrepreneurs blame THEMSELVES for what is actually an infrastructural issue.

- You're not inconsistent — the system is.
- You're not overwhelmed — the operations are.
- You're not unfocused — the workflow is unclear.
- You're not bad at delegating — the documentation is missing.
- You're not struggling — the business is underdeveloped.

Organization is not a personality trait. It is a BUSINESS SKILL. And once you learn it, your entire life gets easier.

Common Mistakes in Stage Six (XP Corrections)

Mistake 1: Hiring without systems

Correction:
Build the SOPs first.

Mistake 2: Growing without KPIs

Correction:
Track numbers weekly.

Mistake 3: Team guessing roles

Correction:
Create role clarity documents.

Mistake 4: Tools before processes

Correction:
Define process → THEN add tools.

Mistake 5: No leadership rhythm

Correction:
Create weekly team structure.

Real Life Application (Implementation Steps)

Step 1: Document 10 Core Processes

Start with sales, fulfillment, and client support.

Step 2: Build Your First Org Chart

Define roles, responsibilities, and reporting.

Step 3: Create Weekly Team Meetings

Each meeting must have an agenda and KPIs.

Step 4: Establish Scorecards

Every team member has 3–5 weekly metrics.

Step 5: Set Up Your Operation Hub

Inside a CRM or project management tool.

Worksheets & Exercises

Exercise 1: The Chaos → Clarity Audit

List all areas of mess.
Rewrite the organized version.

Exercise 2: SOP Builder

Pick one task → document every step.

Exercise 3: Org Chart Planner

List who you have and who you need.

Exercise 4: Leadership Journal Prompts

- What kind of leader do I need to become?
- Where do I avoid structure?
- What systems would free me immediately?

Closing Motivation

Stage Six is the most TRANSFORMATIONAL stage of your business journey.

Because this is the moment you shift from:

- hustler → CEO
- creator → operator
- visionary → leader
- worker → architect
- chaos → control
- pressure → power

This stage is where your business starts feeling like a real company, one that can support you, your family, your team, and your legacy. Once you organize your business, you are finally ready for Stage Seven, the final stage of exponential growth.

Stage Seven is where your business truly becomes a machine that can scale with or WITHOUT you.

CHAPTER 7

STAGE SEVEN - SCALE ($1M → MULTI-MILLION)

The Expansion Stage: Build a Self-Sustaining Enterprise That Outgrows You

You made it.
This is the stage every entrepreneur dreams about but very few reach.

Not because they aren't capable.
Not because they lack talent or ambition.
Not because their vision isn't strong enough.

But because most entrepreneurs never build the foundation required to reach true scale. You did.

You've gone through:

- Energize
- Monetize
- Stabilize
- Productize
- Amplify
- Organize

Now you're ready for the final transformation:

Scale where your business becomes big enough, structured enough, systemized enough, and POWERFUL enough to expand without your constant involvement.

Scaling is not about "more." Scaling is about multiplying what works.

It's not about increasing pressure.

It's about increasing infrastructure.

It's not about working harder.

It's about building smarter.

It's not about doing more.

It's about leading more.

Scaling is the stage where you shift from:

Operator → Owner.
Leader → Legacy Builder.
Entrepreneur → Enterprise.

Welcome to Stage Seven.

Opening Story:

The Real Moment I Knew My Business Was Scaling

There was a moment, a small moment, that changed everything for me. I woke up, checked my phone, and saw:

- sales made
- clients onboarded
- tasks completed
- content posted
- customer support handled
- systems running
- metrics updated
- team communicating
- operations moving

And I had done none of it. Not because I was disconnected. But because I had finally built something that could run without my constant input.

That was the moment I realized:

"My business is no longer ME, it's a MACHINE."

Not a hustle.
Not a job I created for myself.
Not a never-ending workload.

A real business.
A real enterprise.
A real system.
A real organization.

That feeling is what Stage Seven gives you.

And it is one of the most freeing feelings an entrepreneur can experience.

Big Idea of Stage Seven:

A Scalable Business Is a Business That Can Grow Without You

Scaling is NOT:

- more marketing
- more offers
- more stress
- more hours
- more chaos
- more pressure

Scaling IS:

✓ more systems
✓ more leadership
✓ more forecasting
✓ more delegation
✓ more team development
✓ more organizational power
✓ more operational maturity
✓ more automation

- ✓ more metrics
- ✓ more infrastructure
- ✓ more VALUE delivered at scale

Scaling is *freedom through structure.*

Scaling is *growth through duplication.*

Scaling is *expansion through systems.*

Scaling is *volume without pressure.*

If you don't have structure, growth will crush you. If you DO have structure, growth will elevate you. This stage is where your discipline, your system-building, your productizing, and your leadership come together to create something MASSIVE.

Real Life XP Principle #7:

Scale is not the reward.

Scale is the RESULT of structure. People think: "I'm going to get big, then I'll add systems." But real CEOs know: "I add systems so I CAN get big." Scaling is simply THE NATURAL OUTCOME of mastering the first six stages.

If you've built the foundation correctly, scaling feels smooth. If you skipped steps, scaling feels suffocating.

This is why The Seven Stages of Scaling™ matter.
This is why the Real Life OS matters.
This is why your discipline matters.

You cannot scale what you have not organized.
You cannot amplify what you have not productized.
You cannot productize what you have not stabilized.
You cannot stabilize what you have not monetized.
You cannot monetize what you have not energized.

Scaling is the final evolution, not the first.

The Real Life XP Scaling Framework (L.E.G.A.C.Y.)

This framework turns your business into a long-term enterprise:

L - Leadership Expansion

Scaling requires stronger leadership.

You develop:

- department leads
- managers
- coaches
- support staff
- advisors
- directors

You stop being the only leader and start leading leaders.

E - Enterprise-Level Systems

Your software and infrastructure evolve:

- advanced CRM setup
- automated workflows
- division-specific SOPs
- enterprise communication channels
- multi-department dashboards
- forecasting tools
- data reports

Your systems become bigger than the business you started.

G - Growth Through Delegation

At this stage, you delegate to:

- experts
- specialists
- managers
- team leads

You let go of control
and focus on vision, strategy, and leadership.

A - Acquisition & Partnerships

Scaling businesses grow through:

- partnerships
- acquisitions
- collaborations
- franchising opportunities
- licensing
- affiliate networks
- distribution channels

Your business grows with leverage,
not labor.

C - Culture Development

Culture becomes your engine:

- values
- rituals
- communication style
- accountability rhythm
- hiring philosophy
- leadership expectations

Culture is how your business stays strong
even as it gets big.

Y - Your Role Redefined

At this level, your role changes dramatically:

You stop being:

- the operator
- the technician
- the go-to person

- the main problem-solver
- the bottleneck

And you become:

- visionary
- strategist
- relationship-builder
- culture architect
- growth leader

This is when your business finally feels like FREEDOM.

Coach JP Insight (Raw Truth):

You don't scale by adding pressure.

You scale by adding PEOPLE, PROCESSES, and POWER. If scaling feels heavy, you're doing it wrong. Scaling is not about you working harder, it's about you working differently. It's about letting go.

✓ Trusting your systems.
✓ Trusting your team.
✓ Trusting your method.
✓ Trusting the process.
✓ Trusting your leadership.
✓ Trusting your structure.

Scaling requires emotional maturity, not just operational maturity. When you grow internally as a leader, your business grows externally as an enterprise.

Common Mistakes in Stage Seven (XP Corrections)

Mistake 1: Trying to stay the "center" of the business

Correction:
Promote yourself to CEO. Let the machine run.

Mistake 2: Under-hiring

Correction:
Hire leaders, not helpers.

Mistake 3: Micro-managing

Correction:
If you built the system right, trust it.

Mistake 4: Focusing on growth instead of forecasting

Correction:
Scaling requires PREDICTING the future, not reacting to it.

Mistake 5: Expanding without culture

Correction:
Culture holds companies together when pressure hits.

Real Life Application (Implementation Steps)

Step 1: Build a Leadership Team

Identify:

- Head of operations
- Marketing lead
- Client success lead
- Finance manager

Step 2: Automate 70% of Operations

Your systems should handle the bulk.

Step 3: Establish Quarterly Business Planning

Vision → goals → KPIs → accountability.

Step 4: Expand Delivery Capacity

Through coaches, instructors, or specialists.

Step 5: Build Out Your Company Culture Handbook

Document the identity of the company you're becoming.

Worksheets & Exercises

Exercise 1: CEO Time Audit

What tasks must you STOP doing?

Exercise 2: Enterprise Org Chart

What roles will exist at $1M? At $3M? At $10M?

Exercise 3: Scaling Forecast Map

Plan revenue, hires, and systems for the next 12 months.

Exercise 4: Leadership Evolution Journal

- Who must I become to scale?
- What habits must I upgrade?
- What must I release control over?

Closing Motivation

This is the final stage. The elite stage. The stage where very few entrepreneurs ever reach, not because they aren't capable, but because they never built the path.

You did.

✓ You built the structure.
✓ You built the system.

- ✓ You built the clarity.
- ✓ You built the engine.
- ✓ You built the team.
- ✓ You built the authority.
- ✓ You built the momentum.

And now?

You're building the empire.

Scaling is not the end of your journey.

Scaling is the beginning of the legacy you're leaving. Because you didn't just build a business:

- ✓ You built a blueprint.
- ✓ You built an example.
- ✓ You built a generational turning point.
- ✓ You built something REAL.

CONCLUSION

THE FINAL WORD:

Your Future Is Built on the Decisions You Make Next

If you've made it to the end of this book, then you are not just a business owner, you are a builder.

A fighter.
A visionary.
A leader in the making.
A person refusing to settle for "average," "stagnant," "busy," or "stuck."

Most people will never understand what it takes to build something real.
Most people will never see the internal battles you fought.
Most people will never appreciate the discipline, courage, and faith it takes to build a business from scratch, especially as a minority entrepreneur navigating challenges others don't even think about.

But you do. And you showed up for yourself in a way most people never will.

You've studied the path.
You've understood the steps.
You've learned the sequence.
You've embraced the truth:

Business success is not random.

- **It's not luck.**
- **It's not magic.**
- ✓ **It's STRUCTURE.**

- ✓ **It's SEQUENCE.**
- ✓ **It's STRATEGY.**
- ✓ **It's SYSTEMS.**

Now your question becomes:

What will you do with this knowledge?

You Have Three Choices

As you turn this final page, the path becomes clear.

You can:

1. Do nothing

Close this book, go back to life as usual, and hope things eventually "work out."

(They won't. Not without structure.)

2. Try to figure it out alone

Spend years piecing together strategies, frameworks, and systems from random sources.

(You'll make progress, but slowly. And painfully.)

3. Or you can do what hundreds of entrepreneurs have done before you

and get the guidance, systems, and accountability needed to move faster, smarter, and stronger. (This is where exponential progress - XP - truly begins.)

Why You Should Join the Real Life XP 6-Week Coaching Program

The Real Life XP Coaching Program isn't just another course. It isn't a generic program. It's not cookie-cutter. It's not fluff.

It is a **structured, battle-tested, minority-centered, real-life-built system** designed to help entrepreneurs who:

- ✓ are tired of guessing
- ✓ want clarity and direction
- ✓ need real systems and real processes
- ✓ want accountability
- ✓ want to scale sustainably
- ✓ want someone who understands REAL LIFE challenges
- ✓ want to build something that produces stability and success

And it's all rooted in both frameworks you've just read:

- **The Seven Pillars of Real Life XP** (Book 1)
- **The Seven Stages of Scaling™** (Book 2)

These aren't theories they are the exact blueprints I've used to grow Real Life Business Solutions and help entrepreneurs achieve clarity, consistency, and exponential growth.

If you want to:

- Find the gaps in your business
- Fix the problems that are slowing you down
- Build the right systems
- Increase your revenue
- Strengthen your mindset
- Improve your consistency
- Stop the chaos
- And create predictable success

then the coaching program is your next step.

What Happens in the 6-Week Coaching Program

You will work directly with me **Coach JP (Alvin C. Hill IV, MBA)** inside a high-accountability environment designed to create REAL progress in REAL time.

Together, we will:

- Audit your business
- Build clarity around your offer, audience, and model
- Strengthen your mindset and discipline
- Create systems and processes
- Streamline your operations
- Set future goals and structure
- Develop lead generation and marketing rhythms
- Implement the exact steps to reach the next stage of scaling
- Build your personalized "Real Life OS"
- Install the foundations for long-term, sustainable success

This isn't passive learning - this is transformation through action, accountability, and structure.

XP = Exponential Progress

Remember what I told you:

- XP is the opposite of linear progress.
- Linear progress is slow.
- One step at a time.
- Minimal growth.
- Unpredictable outcomes.
- XP is exponential.
- It doubles.
- It compounds.
- It multiplies.

XP is the result of:

- ✓ the right structure
- ✓ the right sequence
- ✓ the right systems
- ✓ the right support
- ✓ and the right coach

You can have exponential results, but only if you make exponential decisions.

This Is Your Moment

You've learned the map.
You've learned the pillars.
You've learned the stages.
You've learned the systems.

Now it's time to install them.

You can do it alone but why would you?

You deserve guidance.
You deserve clarity.
You deserve support.
You deserve accountability.
You deserve to build your dream the RIGHT way, the FAST way, the REAL LIFE way.

Don't let this be another "good book" you finish and forget.
Let this be the turning point in your entrepreneurial journey.

Your Next Step:

Sign Up for the Real Life XP 6-Week Program

If you're ready to shift from information to implementation, from reading to results, from potential to progress

Then go here right now:

www.RealLifeXP.com

1. Complete the form.
2. Submit your information.
3. Book your Clarity Call.
4. Join the program.
5. Get the support.
6. Build the system.
7. Scale the business.
8. Transform your life.

Your future is waiting, but it won't wait forever.

Answer the call.

Step into your next level.

Let's build your XP.

— Coach JP
Founder, Real Life Business Solutions
Creator of The Real Life XP Framework & The Real Life OS
Detroit-Built. Discipline-Forged. Purpose-Driven.

BOOK 3

THE SEVEN GROWTH GEARS

How to Tune, Strengthen, and Accelerate Every Part of Your Business

Alvin C. Hill IV, MBA (Coach JP)

TABLE OF CONTENTS

INTRODUCTION

WHY MOST BUSINESSES NEVER GROW

And Why This Book Gives You the Blueprint to Build a Machine That Can't Collapse

There's a painful truth about entrepreneurship that most people won't tell you:

Businesses don't fail because of a lack of effort. They fail because their gears don't turn. You can be motivated, skilled, creative, and committed, but if even ONE gear in your business is jammed, broken, or grinding: Your growth stops, your confidence drops, your systems buckle, your revenue becomes inconsistent, your stress skyrockets, and you start questioning yourself.

Maybe you've felt this:

- Some months feel smooth.
- Other months feel chaotic.
- Some weeks, your business flows.
- Other weeks, it feels stuck.
- Sometimes you're confident.
- Sometimes you're exhausted.

And none of it seems predictable. You're not alone. And you're not the problem. Most entrepreneurs especially minority entrepreneurs navigating REAL LIFE are never taught the mechanics of growth.

- They're taught to hustle.
- They're taught to grind.

- They're taught to stay dedicated.
- They're taught to "want it more."

But nobody teaches them:

- ✓ how their business actually works
- ✓ how the parts connect
- ✓ how systems affect sales
- ✓ how mindset affects money
- ✓ how team affects time
- ✓ how delivery affects reputation
- ✓ how credibility affects demand
- ✓ how tech affects growth
- ✓ how financial structure affects sustainability

That's why I created **The Seven Growth Gears™**.

Where This Framework Came From

- I didn't learn this from textbooks.
- I didn't learn this from business school.
- I didn't learn this from theory.

I learned it from:

- ✓ being a minority entrepreneur
- ✓ building from scratch
- ✓ starting with nothing
- ✓ overcoming my own internal and external battles
- ✓ failing forward
- ✓ paying for courses that didn't address my REAL LIFE problems
- ✓ coaching entrepreneurs who felt lost, overwhelmed, or stuck
- ✓ studying what makes businesses scale and what makes them collapse

After I created Real Life XP, after I built The Seven Pillars, after I mapped The Seven Stages of Scaling. I realized entrepreneurs needed ONE more thing:

A mechanical blueprint for how the parts of a business actually function together.

Not just:

What should I do next?

But:

1. What gear is broken, and how do I fix it?
2. What gear is strong, and how do I use it to accelerate?
3. What gear is slowing me down without me even noticing?
4. How do I get all seven gears to turn together smoothly?

That's what this book does.

Why XP Is Built on Gears (Not Goals)

Most books teach goals:

- make more money
- get more clients
- improve your brand
- hire a team
- scale your business

But goals don't move businesses.
GEARS do.

- Gears create movement.
- Gears create power.
- Gears create consistency.
- Gears create acceleration.
- Gears create control.
- Gears create sustainability.

A business with one strong gear and six weak ones will always struggle. A business with seven tuned gears becomes unstoppable.

Linear Growth vs. XP Growth (Exponential Progress)

Just like in Books 1 and 2, everything I teach comes back to XP - Exponential Progress. Why? Because linear progress is slow, frustrating, and unpredictable.

Linear growth is:

- one step at a time
- try harder
- do more
- hustle more hours
- grind with more pressure
- hope for more results

But XP growth is different.

XP growth is:

- systems working together
- gears turning smoothly
- momentum compounding
- automation reducing workload
- team multiplying your impact
- clarity increasing speed
- structure eliminating chaos

XP forces you to:

✓ think differently
✓ create systems
✓ build infrastructure
✓ document processes
✓ automate intelligently
✓ hire strategically
✓ lead effectively
✓ plan long-term

XP growth transforms your business from a hustle into a machine.

Who This Book Is For

This book is built specifically for entrepreneurs who:

- feel stuck or overwhelmed
- keep hitting plateaus
- want predictable growth
- want better systems and processes
- want stronger structure
- want a business that grows without burning them out
- are tired of relying on luck
- are ready for clarity
- want a real roadmap
- want a business that feels organized, controlled, and scalable

And especially for entrepreneurs who:

- didn't grow up around business owners
- don't have mentors
- didn't inherit a blueprint
- were taught to grind but not to systemize
- have REAL LIFE responsibilities kids, jobs, bills, trauma, stress, and pressure are building a business with the odds stacked against them

This book is for you. Because your path is different. Your challenges are different. Your obstacles are different. Your needs are different.

And this book honors that.

How This Book Works

Just like Books 1 and 2, this book is structured for learning AND implementation.

Each chapter includes:

- A powerful opening story
- A clear explanation of the gear
- Symptoms when the gear is broken
- XP Pillars that fix the gear
- The official "Growth Gear Framework"

- Common mistakes
- Implementation steps
- Worksheets
- Reflection prompts
- A motivational closing section

Your job is simple:

1. Identify which gears are strong
2. Identify which gears are slipping
3. Strengthen the gears that are holding you back
4. Get all seven gears turning together

When your gears align, your business becomes:

- smoother
- faster
- more predictable
- more profitable
- easier to run
- easier to grow
- easier to scale

And YOU feel more:

- confident
- calm
- grounded
- organized
- powerful
- in control

This is what REAL LIFE business mastery feels like.

Welcome to the Gear System.

Welcome to the Mechanical Blueprint of Growth. Welcome to XP Business Engineering. Your business is a machine. And after this book, you'll finally know how to drive it.

CHAPTER 1
THE FOUNDATION GEAR

Your Personal Readiness, Operational Stability, and Financial Health

Every business problem is rooted in one of two places:

1. The business structure, or
2. The entrepreneur's foundation.

Most people try to fix the business with tactics:

- new marketing
- new pricing
- new funnel
- new website
- new offer

But if the foundation isn't right…

Nothing works.
Nothing sticks.
Nothing scales.

This is why The Foundation Gear sits at the very front of the system because it controls the speed, direction, and stability of every other gear. Before the business grows:

YOU must grow

- ✓ Your habits.
- ✓ Your mindset.
- ✓ Your systems.

- ✓ Your boundaries.
- ✓ Your routines.
- ✓ Your structure.
- ✓ Your financial clarity.
- ✓ Your operational readiness.

If this gear is broken, nothing else turns.

Opening Story:

The Season I Tried to Grow a Business While My Foundation Was Falling Apart:

There was a season in my life where I felt like I was doing everything right:

- working long hours
- staying busy
- grinding every day
- taking on clients
- responding to everyone
- doing all the tasks

but nothing was moving.

- My business wasn't growing.
- My income wasn't consistent.
- My progress didn't match my effort.
- My stress was skyrocketing.
- My confidence kept collapsing.

And I couldn't figure out why.

Until one day, I looked at my calendar, my finances, my routines, my discipline, and I realized something painfully honest:

I wasn't building a business.
I was trying to outrun my lack of foundation.

My:

- mindset was all over the place
- time management was sloppy
- finances were unpredictable
- systems were nonexistent
- documentation was missing
- discipline was inconsistent
- habits were reactive

I wasn't unstable because the business was heavy the business was heavy because **I** was unstable. That's the moment I learned:

You can't scale chaos.

- Before I could elevate, I had to stabilize.
- Before I could grow, I had to strengthen.

Before the business could become more powerful, I had to become more intentional. This gear changed everything for me, and it will do the same for you.

Big Idea of the Foundation Gear:

The Business Can Only Grow at the Speed of the Entrepreneur

Your business is NOT separate from you. It is a reflection of you.

Your business magnifies your:

- discipline
- clarity
- organization
- fear
- insecurity
- habits
- inconsistency
- confidence
- mindset
- emotional state

If you are scattered, your business will be scattered.
If you are unfocused, your business will be unfocused.
If you are inconsistent, your business will be inconsistent.
If you are unstable, your business will be unstable.

This gear answers the most important growth question: **Are YOU ready for growth? Not just the business YOU?** Because if the entrepreneur isn't ready, neither is the business.

When This Gear Is Broken (Symptoms)

You will feel:

- overwhelmed
- burned out
- anxious
- unclear
- stuck
- reactive
- chaotic

Your business will show:

- poor cash flow
- inconsistent income
- emotional decision-making
- disorganization
- lack of structure
- weak credibility
- missing documents
- operational chaos

Your LIFE will show:

- stress
- lack of balance
- mental fatigue
- constant pressure

- unhealthy habits
- no boundaries

When this gear fails, it throws the entire machine off balance.

XP Pillars That Fix This Gear

Three pillars restore this gear:

1. Mindset & Motivation

You must build mental discipline, emotional control, and internal strength.

2. Business Formation & Systems

You must create order, structure, documentation, and organization.

3. Legacy & Impact

You must build long-term clarity and purpose so your decisions align with your future.

Together, these pillars create a strong foundation that ELIMINATES chaos and REPLACES it with stability.

The Foundation Gear Framework (S.T.A.B.L.E.)

To optimize this gear, you must strengthen six areas:

S: Self-Management (Habits, Routines, Focus)

You need:

- a morning routine
- a work rhythm
- task prioritization
- personal discipline
- emotional regulation
- boundary-setting

Self-management is the FIRST leadership skill.

T -Time Control (Not Time Management)

Time management is scheduling tasks.
Time **control** is controlling your energy, focus, and priority.

You need:

- weekly planning
- CEO days
- time blocks
- deep work sessions
- distraction elimination

Your productivity is the KEY to momentum.

A - Administrative Order (Documents, Structure, Credibility)

Your business must be:

- legit
- compliant
- documented
- organized
- protected

This includes:

- LLC
- EIN
- bank accounts
- bookkeeping
- insurance
- contracts
- SOPs
- CRM setup

Credibility creates confidence for you AND the market.

B - Business Finances (Money Stability)

You need control of:

- cash flow

- pricing
- savings
- credit
- taxes
- funding readiness

Money problems are FOUNDATION problems.

L - Life Structure (Boundaries, Balance, Emotional Health)

Your personal life directly affects your business life.

You need:

- boundaries
- support
- clarity
- rest
- mental health practices
- emotional intelligence

You cannot run a high-performance business
with a low-performance lifestyle.

E - Execution Rhythm (Consistency & Action Discipline)

Your execution must be predictable.

- daily actions
- weekly targets
- monthly audits
- quarterly goals

Consistency creates confidence.
Confidence creates momentum.
Momentum creates growth.

Coach JP Insight (Raw Truth):

Your business is not stressed, YOU are stressed.

Your business is not overwhelmed, YOU are overwhelmed. Your business isn't lacking clarity, YOU are. And that's not an insult, it's a revelation. Because if the problem is you, then the solution is also you. And that means you have FULL control of your next level.

The moment you fix this gear, everything else suddenly becomes easier:

- marketing
- sales
- delivery
- operations
- leadership
- scaling

A strong foundation turns struggle into strategy.

Common Mistakes When This Gear Is Broken (XP Corrections)

Mistake 1: Trying to scale while emotionally unstable

Correction:
Fix your foundation before adding more pressure.

Mistake 2: Operating without documented systems

Correction:
Create SOPs for EVERY repeated task.

Mistake 3: Hustling instead of structuring

Correction:
Blocks, routines, and workflows > raw effort.

Mistake 4: Ignoring personal habits

Correction:
Discipline is the foundation of success.

Mistake 5: Avoiding financial organization

Correction:
Money Clarity = Business Clarity.

Real Life Application (Implementation Steps)

Step 1: Conduct a Foundation Audit

Rate yourself 1–10 on:

- discipline
- structure
- organization
- finances
- routines
- mindset

Step 2: Build Your Daily CEO Routine

A 15–30-minute routine that sets your direction for the day.

Step 3: Create Your Admin Folder

Organize all business documents, accounts, and credentials.

Step 4: Set Weekly Non-Negotiable Rhythms

- money check-in
- CRM review
- task planning
- SOP updates

Step 5: Establish Boundary Rules

Protect your mental and emotional bandwidth.

Worksheets & Exercises

Exercise 1: Life & Business Alignment Map

Write what the "stable version of you" looks like.

Exercise 2: Foundation Checklist

Mark off your formation, financial, and operational essentials.

Exercise 3: Habit Builder

Choose 3 habits to strengthen over the next 30 days.

Exercise 4: Foundation Journal Prompts

- What habits are hurting my progress?
- What habits will elevate my progress?
- Where am I operating emotionally instead of strategically?
- What would the grounded, disciplined version of me do next?

Closing Motivation

This gear is the FIRST gear because YOU are the FIRST engine. The business will only ever be as strong, stable, and structured as the entrepreneur leading it.

Once you fix this gear:

✓ your mind becomes clear
✓ your decisions become stronger
✓ your operations become organized
✓ your finances become predictable
✓ your confidence becomes unshakeable

A strong foundation unlocks ALL growth.

Now that YOU are stable, you're ready for the next gear: **the market.**

CHAPTER 2
THE MARKET GEAR

Your Brand Identity, Messaging, Positioning, and Demand in the Marketplace

Your business can have the best systems, the best product, and the best intentions, but if the MARKET doesn't recognize your value, your business will always struggle to grow.

The Market Gear determines:

- how visible your business is
- how attractive your brand feels
- how clear your offer is
- how strongly your audience connects with you
- how confidently prospects choose YOU over competitors
- how many people pay attention
- how many people take action?

When this gear is weak, **your business becomes invisible.**

When this gear is strong, **your business becomes magnetic.**

Visibility, positioning, and messaging are not "nice to have." They are the heart of demand creation. Let's break it down.

Opening Story:

The Era When My Business Was Good but My Market Presence Was Weak

There was a time when:

- my systems were improving
- my offer was strong
- my results were real
- my clients loved the experience

but I still wasn't growing the way I expected. I kept saying:

More people need to hear me.
More people need to see what I do.
More people need this solution.

But here's the truth: The market didn't understand me. Not because I wasn't good at what I did, but because my brand wasn't communicating it clearly

My messaging was too vague.
My content was too inconsistent.
My positioning wasn't defined.
My brand voice wasn't sharpened.
My visuals weren't aligned.
My strategy wasn't intentional.

I was doing the work, but I wasn't telling the story. And in business, the market doesn't respond to effort. The market responds to clarity.

Once I refined my brand, tightened my messaging, and became consistent with my presence, Everything shifted.

People stopped scrolling.
People started listening.
People started reaching out.
People started recognizing me.
People started choosing me.

The Market Gear unlocked visibility, trust, and demand and the business followed.

Big Idea of The Market Gear:

You Cannot Sell What the World Cannot See or Understand

If your business isn't growing, it's probably not because:

- your offer is bad
- your system is weak
- your skills aren't strong
- your product doesn't work

It's usually because of ONE thing: **Your market can't clearly understand your value.**

Not in a confusing way.
Not in a "they'll figure it out" way.
Not in a "well, if they look hard enough" way.

Clarity is the currency of marketing.
Positioning is the engine of demand.
Brand identity is the first form of trust.

This gear answers the question:

Do the right people KNOW you,
GET you,
and CHOOSE you?

If the answer is no,
no amount of strategy fixes it.

When This Gear Is Broken (Symptoms)

You'll notice:

- people don't understand what you do
- you blend in with competitors
- your content doesn't convert
- your brand has no clear identity
- your messaging feels inconsistent
- people say "let me think about it"
- your offer doesn't attract demand
- your audience doesn't grow
- you feel invisible online
- your leads feel random, not predictable

When the Market Gear slips, the entire business slows down.

XP Pillars That Fix This Gear

Two powerful pillars restore this gear:

1. Marketing & Branding

This pillar clarifies your identity, voice, message, offer, positioning, and visibility.

2. Leadership & Team Building

This pillar shapes your brand's tone, confidence, presence, and authority. Without these two pillars, your marketing will always feel confusing or ineffective.

The Market Gear Framework (C.L.E.A.R.)

To strengthen this gear, your brand must become **CLEAR**:

C - Clarity of Audience

Who do you help?

- What do they want?
- What do they fear?
- What do they struggle with?
- What transformation do they crave?

Unclear audience = unclear marketing.

L - Language of Messaging

Do you speak the language of your ideal customer?

Your audience must read your content and think:

> THIS is exactly how I feel.
> THIS person understands me.
> THIS is what I've been looking for.

Clear language = emotional connection.

E - Emotional Positioning

What makes your brand FEEL different?

This includes:

- your tone
- your voice
- your confidence
- your leadership presence
- your authenticity
- your story

People buy emotionally first, logically second.

A - Authority Identity

Why should people trust YOU?

This is built with:

- testimonials
- results
- frameworks
- experience
- values
- consistency

Authority makes buying easy.

R - Relevance in the Marketplace

Are you speaking to TODAY'S problems?

Markets change.
Platforms change.
Culture changes.

A relevant brand stays ahead.

Coach JP Insight (Raw Truth):

If people don't understand your value, they cannot buy your value. You might be the best in your industry but the market doesn't reward the best.

The market rewards the:

- ✓ clearest
- ✓ loudest
- ✓ most consistent
- ✓ most confident
- ✓ best positioned

You cannot serve quietly.
You cannot lead silently.
You cannot win invisibly.

Visibility is your responsibility.
Authority is your advantage.
Brand clarity is your breakthrough.

Common Mistakes When This Gear Is Broken (XP Corrections)

Mistake 1: Talking to "everyone"

Correction: Choose ONE audience.

Mistake 2: Weak messaging

Correction: Name the pain. Promise the transformation.

Mistake 3: Copying competitors

Correction: Build YOUR unique positioning.

Mistake 4: Inconsistent content

Correction: Set a weekly rhythm.

Mistake 5: Being "low-key" out of fear

Correction: Leadership requires visibility.

Real Life Application (Implementation Steps)

Step 1 - Define Your Core Customer

Create a simple profile of who you serve.

Step 2 - Build Your Market Message

One message. One offer. One transformation.

Step 3 - Create Your Brand Identity Map

Tone
Voice
Values
Promise
Personality

Step 4 - Establish Your Weekly Visibility Plan

4–6 pieces of content / week.

Step 5 - Build Your "Authority File"

Store every testimonial, result, review, and win.

Worksheets & Exercises

Exercise 1: Audience Clarity Map

Who do you help?
What do they want?
What is stopping them?

Exercise 2: Market Message Builder

Fill in:

"I help ______ achieve ______ without ______."

Exercise 3: Story Vault

List 10 stories from your life or clients that demonstrate your authority.

Exercise 4: Market Gear Journal Prompts

- What makes my brand truly unique?
- What message do I want the world to hear from me?
- Where am I hiding my authority?
- How can I show up more boldly?

Closing Motivation

The Market Gear is your spotlight. It is your megaphone. It is your signal to the world that:

- ✓ I am here.
- ✓ I am capable.
- ✓ I am relevant.
- ✓ I am the solution.

With a strong Market Gear:

- clients find you
- sales become easier
- content becomes clearer
- your brand becomes magnetic
- your message becomes powerful
- your confidence becomes contagious

Now that the market sees you, you're ready for the next gear: **LEADS.**

CHAPTER 3
THE LEAD GEAR

Your Ability to Generate Predictable, Consistent Inbound & Outbound Demand

You can have the best brand, the best message, and the best offer, but if you don't have consistent, predictable leads, your revenue will always feel shaky. The Lead Gear determines whether your business grows with confidence or operates in fear.

No leads → no conversations
No conversations → no sales
No sales → no growth
No growth → no business

This gear fuels **all** momentum. If it turns, everything else moves. If it slips, everything else struggles. Lead generation is not a luxury it is the oxygen of business.

Opening Story:

The Year My Business Survived on Hope Instead of a Pipeline:

I remember the exact year I realized I wasn't running a real business, I was running a hope machine.

Every week I was hoping someone would reach out.

Hoping someone would find my content.
Hoping someone would DM me.
Hoping someone would refer me.
Hoping a lead would magically appear.

I was stressed.
I was anxious.
I was constantly checking my phone.
I was refreshing my inbox.
I was wondering where the next client would come from.

And it hit me:

Hope is not a lead generation strategy.

I didn't have a pipeline I had a prayer line. And that's not how businesses thrive.

So I made a decision:

I would NEVER again rely on luck or randomness to grow my business. I would build a simple, predictable, measurable system that brings leads every week whether I feel like marketing or not. Once I built that system, everything changed:

- I stopped worrying.
- I stopped guessing.
- I stopped forcing.
- I stopped chasing.
- I stopped stressing.

Leads became predictable. Revenue became predictable. Growth became predictable. The Lead Gear gave me power, control, and peace.

Big Idea of the Lead Gear:

If You Can't Consistently Generate Leads, You Can't Grow Period

This is not optional.
This is not advanced.
This is not "only for big businesses."

This is the GEAR that separates:

- struggling entrepreneurs
  FROM
- successful entrepreneurs

Leads are the fuel for:

- sales
- revenue
- marketing success
- growth confidence
- pipeline strength
- strategic decisions
- financial clarity

If your lead flow is inconsistent, your emotions will be inconsistent.

If your emotions are inconsistent, your decision-making will be inconsistent. If your decision-making is inconsistent, your income will be inconsistent. Everything starts with LEADS.

When This Gear Is Broken (Symptoms)

You will notice:

- Not enough people seeing your business
- Slow or stagnant audience growth
- Inconsistent inquiries
- Relying only on referrals
- Random months of "good" and "bad" leads

- No lead magnet
- No marketing engine
- No CRM tracking
- No ads OR unprofitable ads
- No measurable pipeline

This creates:

- stress
- panic
- poor decision-making
- emotional instability
- low confidence

When the lead gear slips, the business starves.

XP Pillars That Fix This Gear

Two XP Pillars bring this gear back to life:

1. Marketing & Branding

Visibility + messaging = attention.

2. Process & Automation

Systems + tracking = predictability.

Without these pillars, the lead gear can never turn smoothly.

The Lead Gear Framework (P.I.P.E.)

To strengthen this gear, you must build a **PIPE** a Predictable, Intentional Pipeline Engine.

P - Platforms That Drive Traffic

Choose **2–3 reliable** traffic sources:

- TikTok

- Instagram
- YouTube
- Facebook
- LinkedIn
- Email
- Partnerships
- SEO
- Paid ads
- Events
- Communities

Traffic = attention.
Attention = opportunity.

I - Infrastructure for Capture

Your business MUST have:

- lead magnets
- landing pages
- opt-in forms
- nurture sequences
- calls-to-action
- booking links
- simple funnels

Traffic WITHOUT capture = wasted opportunity.

P - Pipeline Tracking

Use a CRM or simple spreadsheet:

Track:

- new leads
- follow-up
- engagement
- next action
- pipeline stage
- results

This is where most entrepreneurs fail because you cannot optimize what you do not measure.

E - Engine of Consistency

This is the rhythm that keeps the gear moving:

- weekly content
- weekly promotion
- daily engagement
- regular emails
- partnerships
- follow-up automation
- retargeting campaigns

CONSISTENCY > INTENSITY.

Coach JP Insight (Raw Truth):

Your business isn't slow because you're bad.

It's slow because your lead machine is silent.

It's not a talent problem.
It's not a confidence problem.
It's not a capability problem.

It's a visibility and pipeline problem.

And that's GOOD news because pipeline problems are FIXABLE.

Once you build a predictable lead engine:

- sales become easier
- marketing becomes enjoyable
- growth becomes stable
- confidence becomes stronger
- the business feels lighter

Leads give you **options**.
Options give you **freedom**.

Common Mistakes When This Gear Is Broken (XP Corrections)

Mistake 1: Only doing organic OR only doing paid

Correction: Use a hybrid approach.

Mistake 2: Posting content without a lead capture system

Correction: Always include a CTA.

Mistake 3: Not tracking leads daily

Correction: Use CRM or pipeline sheet.

Mistake 4: Relying on referrals

Correction: Build a marketing engine.

Mistake 5: Inconsistency

Correction: Weekly non-negotiable lead actions.

Real Life Application (Implementation Steps)

Step 1: Choose Your 2 Main Traffic Platforms

Pick where your audience actually hangs out.

Step 2: Create One Strong Lead Magnet

Solve ONE painful problem with a quick win.

Step 3: Build Your Lead Capture System

Landing page → thank you page → funnel → automation.

Step 4: Set a Weekly Lead Rhythm

Example:

- 4 content pieces
- 1 CTA post

- 20 minutes of engagement
- 1 email
- 1 collaboration

Step 5: Use a Pipeline Tracker Daily

Every lead must have:

- a status
- a next step
- a follow-up date

Worksheets & Exercises

Exercise 1: Lead Audit

Where are leads coming from now?
Where do you want them to come from?

Exercise 2: Traffic Source Brainstorm

List all possible visibility channels.

Exercise 3: Lead Magnet Builder

Create a quick-win solution your audience wants immediately.

Exercise 4: Lead Gear Journal Prompts

- Where am I inconsistent with lead generation?
- What platform gives me the best traction?
- What message do I need to amplify?
- What would my business look like with 20 leads per week?

Closing Motivation

The Lead Gear is the **fuel line** of your business.

When this gear turns:

✓ your confidence expands
✓ your sales increase

- ✓ your opportunities multiply
- ✓ your marketing amplifies
- ✓ your business grows with ease

When it slips:

- you feel pressure
- you doubt yourself
- you panic
- you shrink
- your business slows to a crawl

Leads cure doubt.
Leads cure fear.
Leads cure instability.
Leads cure inconsistency.

Strengthen this gear, and the entire machine comes ALIVE.

Now you're ready for the gear that turns leads into MONEY:

The Sales Gear.

CHAPTER 4

THE SALES GEAR

Your System for Turning Leads Into Revenue Consistently

You can have incredible branding, consistent leads, and strong marketing, but if you can't close consistently, your business will ALWAYS feel unstable.

The Sales Gear is the converter gear, the one that transforms attention into income, curiosity into commitment, and conversations into customers.

When this gear turns smoothly, your business feels powerful.

Predictable.
Secure.
Strong.

When this gear slips, everything slows down no matter how good the other gears are.

Sales is not the most important gear, but it is the most sensitive one. Even a small misalignment can jam the entire machine.

Opening Story:

The Moment I Realized I Wasn't "Bad at Sales," I Was Just Unstructured :

For years, I thought I had a sales problem. People would DM me, ask questions, say they were interested but they wouldn't buy.

I assumed:

- My price was too high.
- My audience wasn't serious.
- My offer wasn't appealing.
- My market wasn't ready.
- People didn't understand the value.

But none of that was the issue.

The problem was simple:

I had no predictable, repeatable sales system.

Every conversation was different.
Every call was different.
Every message was different.
Every follow-up was different.

My pipeline wasn't organized.
My follow-up wasn't automated.
My conversations weren't structured.
My offer wasn't clearly positioned.
My objections weren't pre-handled.
My pricing wasn't confidently presented.

I wasn't bad at sales

I was bad at systems.

Once I built a structured, predictable sales process…

- my confidence increased
- my close rate skyrocketed
- my conversations became smoother
- my pipeline became cleaner
- my revenue became consistent

I didn't need to change ME.
I needed to change the SYSTEM. And that's exactly what this gear fixes.

Big Idea of the Sales Gear:

Sales Is NOT About Charm, It's About SYSTEMS

People think sales is:

- convincing
- persuading
- being good with people
- charisma
- hype
- pressure
- personality
- tricks

Sales is NONE of that.

Real, sustainable, predictable sales is:

- structure
- process
- psychology
- consistency
- follow-up
- tracking
- clarity
- confidence

The best salespeople aren't slick they're SYSTEMATIC. They follow a process that works and they repeat it again and again and again. This gear answers the critical question:

Do you have a predictable, repeatable process that turns prospects into clients consistently?

If not, the sales gear is not turning.

When This Gear Is Broken (Symptoms)

Your business will show:

- low close rates
- prospects "thinking about it"
- people ghosting you
- inconsistent revenue
- slow months after good months
- relying on luck
- manual follow-up
- no CRM
- unclear sales process
- offer not converting
- sales calls feel awkward
- owner handles all sales out of necessity
- inconsistent pricing

And YOU will feel:

- pressure
- frustration
- doubt
- confusion
- emotional swings

A broken sales gear drains your confidence AND your bank account.

XP Pillars That Fix This Gear

Three pillars power this gear:

1. Process & Automation

Sales becomes predictable when the system is predictable.

2. Marketing & Branding

Because the best sales process can't fix poor offer positioning.

3. Leadership & Team Building

Because eventually, you'll need sales reps, closers, or setters.

The Sales Gear Framework (C.L.O.S.E.)

This is the Real Life XP blueprint for building a predictable sales system.

C - Clarity of Offer

People don't buy complicated things.

Your offer must be:

- simple
- powerful
- emotionally compelling
- clearly described
- differentiated
- built around one outcome

Confused prospects don't buy.

L - Lead Qualification

Not every lead is a prospect.

Your system must identify:

- who is serious
- who is ready
- who can afford
- who is ideal
- who needs nurture

Qualification saves time and increases conversion.

O - Objection Handling (Pre-Defined)

Most objections are predictable:

- price

- timing
- trust
- spouse
- money
- uncertainty
- let me think about it

These should be handled BEFORE they arise through content, messaging, and process.

S - Sales Script & Structure

Your sales conversations must follow a framework:

1. Build connection
2. Identify pain
3. Define goals
4. Present solution
5. Handle objections
6. Close with clarity

Scripts don't make you robotic.
Scripts make you consistent.

E - Execution & Follow-Up Automation

Most sales don't close immediately.

People buy through:

- drip emails
- SMS follow-up
- retargeting
- pipeline nudges
- reminders
- social proof
- authority building

Most revenue is in the follow-up NOT the first conversation.

Coach JP Insight (Raw Truth):

You don't have a "sales problem."

You have a "sales process problem."

If you were bad at sales, you'd be bad at:

- getting clients
- landing opportunities
- creating relationships
- convincing people
- inspiring others
- building your business

But you're not bad at any of those.

You're just inconsistent because the SYSTEM is inconsistent.

When you fix the system:

- ✓ your income increases
- ✓ your stress decreases
- ✓ your confidence strengthens
- ✓ your pipeline grows
- ✓ your customers convert faster
- ✓ your business becomes predictable

Sales is the easiest gear to fix and the fastest one to transform your business.

Common Mistakes When This Gear Is Broken (XP Corrections)

Mistake 1: "Winging" sales calls

Correction: Follow a script.

Mistake 2: No follow-up

Correction: Automate it.

Mistake 3: Price insecurity

Correction: Sell transformation, not time.

Mistake 4: Waiting for leads to close themselves

Correction: Move prospects through a structured pipeline.

Mistake 5: Not documenting objections

Correction: Build objection-handling content.

Real Life Application (Implementation Steps)

Step 1 - Write Your Sales Script

Use a repeatable framework.

Step 2 - Build Your Follow-Up Automations

3–5 days of reminders.
Then weekly nurture.

Step 3 - Create Offer Clarity Pages

Show transformation, results, and proof.

Step 4 - Set Daily Pipeline Tasks

Check your CRM every day.

Step 5 - Track Close Rate Weekly

If you don't measure it, you can't improve it.

Worksheets & Exercises

Exercise 1: Offer Clarity Worksheet

Write your offer in one sentence.

Exercise 2: Objection Library

List the top 10 objections and your responses.

Exercise 3: Sales Script Builder

Fill in each stage of your conversation flow.

Exercise 4: Sales Gear Journal Prompts

- What part of my sales process feels the weakest?
- What objections do I struggle to handle?
- What would a confident closer version of me do differently?

Closing Motivation

The Sales Gear is where:

- confidence becomes cash
- conversations become commitments
- opportunities become income
- effort becomes results

When this gear turns:

- your revenue stabilizes
- your business strengthens
- your fear fades
- your predictability increases
- your pipeline grows
- your momentum multiplies

Master this gear, and you'll never fear a slow month again. You're ready for the next gear the gear that shapes your reputation and results:

The Delivery Gear.

CHAPTER 5

THE DELIVERY GEAR

Your Client Experience, Fulfillment Systems, and Quality of Service

The hard truth is:

- ✓ You can have perfect branding
- ✓ You can have predictable leads
- ✓ You can have strong sales

but if you can't **deliver results**, your business will:

- lose clients
- lose referrals
- lose trust
- lose retention
- lose credibility
- lose momentum

The Delivery Gear determines whether your business grows *after* the sale not just before it.

This gear is where:

- reputation is built
- results are created
- client experience is shaped
- systems are tested
- chaos becomes clarity
- consistency becomes culture

Delivery is the MOST important gear when it comes to:

- long-term success
- referrals
- client satisfaction
- repeat revenue
- brand loyalty

If this gear slips, your entire business grinds. But when this gear is tuned correctly? You become unbeatable in your market.

Opening Story:

The Era When My Marketing Was Working, but My Delivery Was Drowning Me:

There was a point in my business where:

✓ leads were coming in
✓ sales were increasing
✓ revenue was climbing
✓ systems were growing

but behind the scenes, fulfillment was messy.

- Clients were confused.
- Communication was inconsistent.
- Everything was manual.
- Onboarding was unclear.
- I was overworked.
- My team was overwhelmed.
- Nothing was documented.
- Everything was improvised.

The truth was painful:

My business looked strong on the outside but weak on the inside.

And when delivery suffers:

- retention drops

- referrals disappear
- refunds increase
- stress grows
- team morale falls
- client experience collapses

I didn't have a marketing problem. I had a DELIVERY problem.

So I rebuilt the entire backend:

- onboarding flows
- client communication
- SOPs
- fulfillment timelines
- delivery automation
- quality standards
- internal documentation

And once I did?

Clients were happier.
Results were better.
Retention skyrocketed.
Referrals doubled.
Stress disappeared.
Fulfillment scaled.

That's the power of fixing this gear.

Big Idea of The Delivery Gear:

You Don't Have a Real Business Until You Can Deliver Results Consistently

Marketing creates interest.
Sales creates revenue.
But DELIVERY creates longevity.

This gear controls:

- outcomes
- satisfaction
- retention
- referrals
- reputation
- your brand's true identity

You can't scale poor delivery.
You can't automate chaos.
You can't delegate confusion.
You can't grow inconsistency.

This gear asks the tough question:

Do clients get impressive results every time?

Not "sometimes."
Not "when things go smoothly."
Not "when you're not overwhelmed."

Every single time.

If the answer is no,
this gear demands your attention.

When This Gear Is Broken (Symptoms)

The business will show:

- inconsistent client results
- refunds or churn
- confused customers
- slow delivery
- overwhelmed team
- missing SOPs
- unclear onboarding
- messy communication
- everything dependent on the owner

- no quality control
- inconsistent outcomes

YOU will feel:

- stressed
- behind
- overworked
- drained
- frustrated
- unsupported

When delivery fails,
your business reputation crumbles.

XP Pillars That Fix This Gear

Three pillars restore this gear:

1. Process & Automation

You need workflows, systems, and automation.

2. Business Formation & Systems

Backend organization and structure.

3. Leadership & Team Building

Because fulfillment depends on people not just systems.

The Delivery Gear Framework (R.E.S.U.L.T.)

This framework ensures every client receives a premium experience.

R - Rapid & Clear Onboarding

Clients must instantly know:

- what happens next

- how the process works
- what they need to do
- how to communicate
- what to expect

Confusion kills trust early.
Clarity builds confidence.

E - Efficient Fulfillment Systems

You need documented workflows for:

- how services are delivered
- in what order
- by whom
- using what tools
- on what timeline

Consistency creates reliability.

S - Support & Communication Structure

Clients need:

- easy communication
- timely responses
- clear support channels
- expectations
- updates

Communication is part of the product.

U - Unified Client Experience

Your delivery must feel:

- seamless
- smooth
- predictable
- well-designed
- high quality

It should NEVER feel improvised.

L - Leveraged Delivery (Automation + Team)

Automate:

- reminders
- onboarding steps
- check-ins
- content delivery
- instructions
- follow-up

Delegate fulfillment tasks. Stop doing everything manually.

T - Tracking of Outcomes

Measure:

- client progress
- client success
- client satisfaction
- retention
- referral rates

What you track improves.
What you ignore decays.

Coach JP Insight (Raw Truth):

You are not overwhelmed because you have too many clients.

You are overwhelmed because your delivery is unstructured.

The problem isn't volume.
The problem is inconsistency.

If everything depends on you:

- you become the bottleneck
- clients get delayed
- support becomes scattered
- your stress increases

- your quality decreases
- your reputation suffers

When your delivery gear is optimized:

✓ your stress drops
✓ your confidence grows
✓ your team thrives
✓ your clients win
✓ your referrals explode
✓ your brand becomes undeniable

Delivery creates momentum that money can't buy.

Common Mistakes When This Gear Is Broken (XP Corrections)

Mistake 1: Treating fulfillment like an afterthought

Correction: Delivery is the MOST important gear.

Mistake 2: Manual onboarding

Correction: Automate it.

Mistake 3: No SOPs

Correction: Document everything.

Mistake 4: Poor communication

Correction: Build communication rules + channels.

Mistake 5: Owner doing every task

Correction: Delegate and automate.

Real Life Application (Implementation Steps)

Step 1 - Build a Premium Onboarding Flow

Email → SMS → Welcome video → Setup instructions.

Step 2 - Document Your Fulfillment SOPs

Every task, step-by-step.

Step 3 - Automate 30–50% of Delivery

Reminders, instructions, follow-up, access links.

Step 4 - Create a Client Experience Roadmap

Show the entire journey from start to finish.

Step 5 - Build a Support Structure

Slack, email, text, or ticketing system.

Worksheets & Exercises

Exercise 1: Delivery Audit

Where do clients get stuck?
Where do YOU get stuck?

Exercise 2: Onboarding Flow Builder

Map the first 7 days of the client experience.

Exercise 3: SOP Template

Document one process fully.

Exercise 4: Delivery Gear Journal Prompts

- What part of delivery stresses me out most?
- What do clients ask repeatedly?
- How can I automate that?
- Where is my delivery inconsistent?

Closing Motivation

The Delivery Gear is where your business proves itself.

It is where:

- ✓ promises become results
- ✓ clients become advocates
- ✓ satisfaction becomes loyalty
- ✓ quality becomes reputation
- ✓ excellence becomes your advantage

If you master this gear, your clients become your marketing. Your results become your authority.
Your reputation becomes your brand. Strong delivery builds empires.

Now that you can deliver excellence, you're ready for the next gear the one that removes YOU as the bottleneck:

The Team Gear.

CHAPTER 6
THE TEAM GEAR
Your Hiring, Leadership, Delegation, Communication, and Accountability Systems

Every entrepreneur eventually hits the same wall:

You run out of time.
You run out of energy.
You run out of capacity.

No matter how talented, disciplined, or efficient you are, you cannot outwork the limits of being ONE person.

Growth requires support.

Expansion requires people.

Scale requires a TEAM.

The Team Gear determines whether your business becomes:

- a one-person hustle, or
- a sustainable, scalable enterprise

If this gear turns correctly, your business becomes:

- lighter
- faster
- more efficient
- more powerful
- more predictable

- more sustainable

If this gear slips, your business becomes:

- chaotic
- dependent on you
- slow
- stressful
- fragile

This gear is where you transform from "entrepreneur" to **leader**.

Opening Story:

The Moment I Realized I Was the Bottleneck:

For a long time, my problem wasn't:

- leads
- sales
- delivery
- marketing
- systems

My problem was ME.

I was doing everything:

- onboarding
- fulfillment
- replying to emails
- scheduling calls
- handling sales
- updating the CRM
- creating content
- managing clients
- designing graphics
- solving problems
- putting out fires
- staying up late

- waking up drained

I wasn't running a business I was running a **personal labor camp**.

And then one day it hit me:

I'm not overwhelmed because the work is hard. I'm overwhelmed because the work is SOLO.

I didn't need more time.
I needed more people.
I needed delegation.
I needed support.
I needed structure.
I needed leadership.

When I built my first real team everything changed:

- ✓ the business grew faster
- ✓ delivery improved
- ✓ my stress decreased
- ✓ my time increased
- ✓ my confidence soared
- ✓ my impact expanded
- ✓ my systems strengthened

I finally understood:

Scaling is not about doing more. Scaling is about doing less with the right support.

Big Idea of The Team Gear:

You Don't Build a Big Business by Working Harder; You Build It by Leading People Better

The Team Gear is about:

- hiring
- delegation
- training

- leadership
- communication
- accountability
- culture
- roles
- expectations
- structure

Most entrepreneurs fail not because they can't lead, but because they've never BEEN led properly.

This gear teaches you how to:

- choose the right people
- put them in the right roles
- set clear expectations
- measure performance
- develop leadership
- create a culture
- build accountability
- elevate your identity as a CEO

This gear answers the question:

Does your team amplify your results or drain your energy?

When This Gear Is Broken (Symptoms)

A broken team gear looks like:

- you are doing everything
- hiring the wrong people
- high stress
- confusion about roles
- low accountability
- inconsistent performance
- poor communication
- frustration
- delays in delivery

- slow progress
- burnout
- turnover

Your team is not the problem. Your SYSTEMS are the problem.

XP Pillars That Fix This Gear

1. Leadership & Team Building

Guidance. Development. Culture. Communication.

2. Process & Automation

Documented workflows make training easier.

3. Business Formation & Systems

Clear roles. Clear responsibilities. Clear structure.

The Team Gear Framework (L.E.A.D.)

This four-part framework shapes how XP builds teams that scale.

L - Locate the Right People

Hiring is not about talent. It's about FIT.

You need people who match:

✓ your values
✓ your mission
✓ your work ethic
✓ your culture
✓ your communication style
✓ your expectations

A skilled person with the wrong attitude is more dangerous than an unskilled beginner with potential. Hire for alignment. Train for skill.

E - Establish Roles, Rules & Responsibilities

Every team member must know:

- what they do
- how they do it
- when they do it
- why they do it
- how success is measured

If roles are unclear, performance becomes chaotic. If expectations are unclear, communication becomes stressful. If responsibilities are unclear, accountability disappears.

A - Accountability & Performance Tracking

People do what you INSPECT, not what you EXPECT.

You need:

- KPIs
- weekly check-ins
- scorecards
- quarterly goals
- clear deadlines
- deliverable tracking

Accountability is not micromanagement it is alignment.

D - Develop & Delegate

You cannot lead if you cannot let go.

Delegation requires:

- trust
- clarity
- documentation
- patience
- leadership
- confidence

Your job is not to do tasks. Your job is to empower PEOPLE to do tasks. You grow by releasing control not clinging to it.

Coach JP Insight (Raw Truth):

You are not tired because the business is heavy. You are tired because you're carrying it alone. Entrepreneurs stay "solo" out of fear:

- fear no one will care as much
- fear someone will mess it up
- fear of paying people
- fear of letting go
- fear of being a leader
- fear of trusting the wrong person

But here's the REAL fear:

If you don't build a team, you will never build a business.

You will forever be:

- the technician
- the customer service rep
- the marketer
- the sales rep
- the admin worker
- the bookkeeper
- the manager
- the everything

That is not entrepreneurship.
That is enslavement.

Leadership frees you.
Systems support you.
Team strengthens you.

This gear sets you free.

Common Mistakes When This Gear Is Broken (XP Corrections)

Mistake 1: Hiring too fast

Correction: Hire slowly. Fire quickly.

Mistake 2: No documented training

Correction: SOPs + onboarding systems.

Mistake 3: Holding everything inside your head

Correction: Build a centralized operations hub.

Mistake 4: Avoiding tough conversations

Correction: Clear communication builds respect.

Mistake 5: Taking back tasks you delegated

Correction: Fix the process, not the person.

Real Life Application (Implementation Steps)

Step 1: Identify Your First 3 Delegable Tasks

Look for tasks that drain energy or slow growth.

Step 2: Create Job Descriptions for Key Roles

Define what success looks like.

Step 3: Build a Training Library

Screen recordings
Tutorials
Checklists
SOPs

Step 4: Set Weekly Leadership Rhythms

Check-ins
Scorecard reviews
Pipeline updates

Step 5: Build a Culture Code

Values
Expectations
Standards

Worksheets & Exercises

Exercise 1: Team Audit

Where are the bottlenecks?
Where do you need support?

Exercise 2: Role Builder

Define responsibilities for each key role.

Exercise 3: Delegation Map

What can you automate?
What can you delegate?
What must you keep?

Exercise 4: Team Gear Journal Prompts

- What leadership habits must I strengthen?
- What tasks should I stop doing personally?
- What team structure does my next level require?

Closing Motivation

The Team Gear is not just about people it's about identity.

This is where you step into:

- leadership
- confidence
- influence
- vision
- expansion

Because no matter how strong you are individually, **you cannot build something big without others.**

A tuned team gear creates:

- freedom
- scalability
- speed
- stability
- sustainability
- long-term success

And now that you have support…

You're ready for the final gear the gear that transforms your business from stable to scalable:

The Growth Gear.

CHAPTER 7

THE GROWTH GEAR

Your Data, Technology, AI, Capital, and Long-Term Strategy

This is the gear that separates:

- hustlers from builders,
- small businesses from scalable companies,
- operators from CEOs,
- and entrepreneurs from founders.

The Growth Gear is where your business stops being a day-to-day grind and becomes a long-term machine.

This gear governs:

✓ your strategy
✓ your infrastructure
✓ your technology
✓ your automation
✓ your data
✓ your capital
✓ your future

If the earlier gears make the business run, **this gear determines how far it can go.**

This is where you shift from:

- short-term choices → long-term design
- guesswork → data

- emotion → logic
- hustle → systems
- survival → expansion

The Growth Gear isn't about "more." It's about **multiplication.**

Opening Story:

The Moment I Stopped Building a Business, And Started Building an Enterprise:

There was a period where everything was working:

- leads were coming in
- sales were consistent
- delivery was strong
- team was supportive
- systems were in place

I was proud.
I was stable.
I was confident.

But something unexpected happened:

I hit a new kind of plateau, not because things were broken, but because my vision wasn't big enough.

I was running the business like a day-to-day operation, not an expanding enterprise. I had no data dashboard.

No KPI rhythm.

No long-term roadmap.
No funding strategy.
No exit plan.
No scale blueprint.
No growth milestones.
No automation expansion.

I realized something powerful:

You can have a well-running business that still has no future.

That awakening pushed me into the Growth Gear.

I started:

- tracking everything
- using data, not feelings
- optimizing systems
- implementing AI
- building a tech stack
- planning for funding
- creating an expansion roadmap
- designing a multi-year strategy
- preparing for a potential exit

And once I did?

The business stopped surviving and started scaling.

Big Idea of The Growth Gear:

Growth Does Not Happen by Hustle, It Happens by ENGINEERING

Growth is NOT:

- luck
- timing
- hoping
- grinding
- talent
- guessing

Growth is:

✓ structure
✓ technology
✓ measurement

- ✓ capital
- ✓ automation
- ✓ planning
- ✓ leadership
- ✓ future vision

This gear answers the question:

Do you have the systems, data, tools, and strategy to scale sustainably and profitably?

If not, growth is random. When this gear turns, growth becomes predictable.

When This Gear Is Broken (Symptoms)

A business lacking this gear will:

- operate emotionally
- make decisions based on "feelings"
- have inconsistent growth
- struggle with cash flow
- lack data visibility
- move slowly
- rely too much on the owner
- have weak infrastructure
- avoid technology
- lack funding
- have no long-term clarity

This creates:

- stagnation
- burnout
- overwhelm
- fear
- poor decision-making
- missed opportunities

You cannot scale with guesswork. You scale with data and design.

XP Pillars That Fix This Gear

Three pillars empower this gear:

1. Credit & Capital

Funding fuels growth.
Without capital, you plateau.

2. Legacy & Impact

Long-term decisions require long-term thinking.

3. Business Formation & Systems

You need the legal, operational, and structural foundation for expansion.

The Growth Gear Framework (S.C.A.L.E.)

To activate this gear, you must build the SCALING ENGINE of your business.

S - Scorecards & Data Tracking

You must track:

- revenue
- leads
- close rate
- delivery timelines
- churn
- retention
- fulfillment efficiency
- team performance
- marketing metrics

Data is the antidote to emotional decisions.

C - Capital Readiness & Funding Strategy

Growth requires money.

You need:

- business credit
- funding sources
- lines of credit
- loans
- grants
- financial partners

Capital is leverage and leverage accelerates growth.

A - Automation & AI Integration

AI and automation should:

- reduce workload
- increase speed
- improve accuracy
- eliminate manual tasks
- increase consistency
- lower costs
- strengthen delivery
- scale communication
- enhance marketing
- power your CRM

A slow business becomes fast with automation.

L - Long-Term Roadmap

Your business needs a plan for:

- 1 year
- 3 years
- 5 years
- 10 years

This includes:

- growth milestones
- expansion plans
- new offers

- team structure
- financial goals
- market positioning

Without a roadmap,
your business drifts instead of drives.

E - Expansion Strategy & Exit Potential

You must think like a CEO:

- Will you franchise?
- Will you open more offices?
- Will you build a team of leaders?
- Will you create digital products?
- Will you license your IP?
- Will you build to sell?
- Will you pass it down?

Legacy is built through intention, not accident.

Coach JP Insight (Raw Truth):

If you are not tracking data, you are not running a business you are running a guess.

You cannot rely on:

- moods
- feelings
- emotions
- assumptions
- random spikes
- temporary wins

Real CEOs make decisions based on:

✓ metrics
✓ dashboards
✓ capital strategy

- ✓ automation
- ✓ efficiency
- ✓ predictability

Your next level is NOT about working harder. It's about thinking bigger and operating smarter.

This gear is where businesses turn into machines,
and machines turn into empires.

Common Mistakes When This Gear Is Broken (XP Corrections)

Mistake 1: Avoiding technology

Correction: Embrace automation.

Mistake 2: Waiting too long to seek funding

Correction: Build credit early.

Mistake 3: Making decisions emotionally

Correction: Build scorecards.

Mistake 4: No long-term planning

Correction: Build a growth roadmap.

Mistake 5: Growing without infrastructure

Correction: Strengthen systems FIRST.

Real Life Application (Implementation Steps)

Step 1 - Build Your KPI Dashboard

Track your most important numbers weekly.

Step 2 - Map Your Funding Strategy

Identify:

- lenders
- credit accounts
- grants
- capital needs

Step 3 - Automate 20–40% of Your Business

Start with:

- onboarding
- communication
- follow-up
- task management

Step 4 - Design a 3-Year Roadmap

Define:

- revenue milestones
- team structure
- products/services
- system upgrades

Step 5 - Document Your Expansion Vision

Franchise?
License?
Sell?
Scale nationally?
Grow your team?

Worksheets & Exercises

Exercise 1: Growth Audit

Where is your business inefficient or slow?

Exercise 2: KPI Builder

Track your 10 most important metrics.

Exercise 3: Capital Plan

List potential funding sources.

Exercise 4: Growth Gear Journal Prompts

- What does my business look like at scale?
- What's my 3-year vision?
- What's preventing me from growing faster?
- Where do I need automation today?

Closing Motivation

The Growth Gear is where true transformation happens.

This is where you:

- expand
- elevate
- automate
- scale
- optimize
- fund
- strategize
- build your legacy

This gear turns your business into a:

- system
- structure
- machine

- organization
- enterprise

It frees you from survival and positions you for long-term impact.

You've now mastered:

- ✓ your foundation
- ✓ your market identity
- ✓ your lead flow
- ✓ your sales engine
- ✓ your delivery systems
- ✓ your team structure
- ✓ your growth strategy

These seven gears create a machine powerful enough to change your life, your family, your future, and your legacy. Now you're ready for the final pages:

The Conclusion of Book 3.

CONCLUSION

THE FINAL WORD:

Your Growth Isn't an Accident, It's a Gear You Control

If you've made it to this final page, let me tell you something most entrepreneurs never hear:

You are no longer guessing.
You now have the blueprint.
You now understand the machine.
You now control the gears.

Most business owners struggle not because they aren't capable, not because they aren't talented, not because they don't work hard but because they don't know how their business actually functions underneath.

They build from emotion instead of structure.
They grow from reaction instead of intention.
They scale from stress instead of systems.

But **YOU** now see the truth:

- A business is not magic.
- A business is not momentum.
- A business is not motivation.

✓ A business is **mechanical,** and you are now the engineer.

You Now Understand the Seven Growth Gears

You built:

- Stability through the **Foundation Gear**
- Visibility through the **Market Gear**
- Predictability through the **Lead Gear**
- Profitability through the **Sales Gear**
- Reputation through the **Delivery Gear**
- Freedom through the **Team Gear**
- Scalability through the **Growth Gear**

That means you now hold the **operating system** for running a REAL business one that doesn't collapse when life hits,
one that doesn't crumble when pressure rises,
one that doesn't stall when sales slow,
one that doesn't exhaust you trying to keep it alive.

Your business can now:

✓ generate consistent leads
✓ create predictable revenue
✓ deliver strong results
✓ function with a team
✓ operate with systems
✓ expand with strategy
✓ grow with intelligence
✓ scale with intention

This is what REAL entrepreneurship looks like.

Your Life Will Change When Your Gears Align

When the seven gears turn together:

✓ your stress drops
✓ your confidence rises
✓ your revenue becomes reliable
✓ your team becomes empowered

✓ your system becomes organized
✓ your impact expands
✓ your time multiplies

Most importantly you finally feel like the CEO of your life not the employee of your business. This is what exponential progress (XP) is all about.

A Message from Coach JP

Let me speak to you directly,

I created the Real Life XP Program and these Growth Gears because I spent YEARS trying to figure this out the hard way with no guidance, no resources, no blueprint, and no one who understood the REAL LIFE challenges I was facing as a minority entrepreneur.

I don't want you to go through that.
I don't want you to waste years guessing.
I don't want you to struggle in silence.
I don't want you to keep grinding without growth.
I don't want you to keep hitting walls that have simple solutions.

You deserve clarity.
You deserve systems.
You deserve structure.
You deserve support.
You deserve success that lasts not success that stresses.

And if you're reading this, you're someone who takes their business, their future, and their legacy seriously.

So here's my final message:

Don't just read this book.
INSTALL this book.
APPLY the gears.
ALIGN the machine.
ACTIVATE your XP.

Your business and your life will transform.

Your Next Step:

Join the Real Life XP 6-Week Coaching Program

Now that you understand the gears, it's time to build them together. In the Real Life XP Coaching Program, we work side-by-side for six weeks to:

- ✓ audit your entire business
- ✓ tune each of the seven gears
- ✓ strengthen your foundation
- ✓ sharpen your messaging
- ✓ build your lead engine
- ✓ construct your sales systems
- ✓ optimize your delivery
- ✓ document your operations
- ✓ train you to lead a team
- ✓ map your long-term growth plan

Everything you just learned becomes real, tangible, and installed.

This is not just coaching its business engineering.

It's transformation.
It's structure.
It's momentum.
It's exponential progress.

If you're ready for clarity, support, strategy, and RESULTS…

Go to www.RealLifeXP.com
Complete the form
Join the 6-week program

Your next level is waiting but it won't wait forever.

The gears are in your hands now.
Turn them with confidence.
Turn them with discipline.
Turn them with intention.
Turn them with purpose.

You have everything you need. Now go build what's yours.

— Coach JP (Alvin C. Hill IV, MBA)
Founder, Real Life Business Solutions
Creator of The Real Life XP Framework & The Seven Growth Gears
Detroit-Built. Legacy-Focused. Purpose-Driven.

SUMMARY

REAL LIFE DOESN'T HAND OUT BLUEPRINTS.
SO I BUILT ONE.

Every entrepreneur wants growth, but most were never taught *how* to build it. The Real Life XP Growth Engine is a complete, battle-tested system designed for real people facing real challenges, building real businesses in the real world.

This powerful volume brings together all three core frameworks of the Real Life XP system:

BOOK 1: The Seven Pillars of Real Life XP

Develop the mindset, discipline, identity, and inner foundation required to become the entrepreneur your business needs.

BOOK 2: The Seven Stages of Scaling

See exactly where you are in the business growth journey and follow the step-by-step roadmap to move from survival to stability to scale.

BOOK 3: The Seven Growth Gears

Tune, strengthen, and accelerate every core part of your business—marketing, sales, operations, systems, leadership, and growth levers.

WHY THIS MATTERS

Before building Real Life Business Solutions into a multiple six-figure company, **Alvin C. Hill IV, MBA** also known as **Coach JP** faced financial setbacks, personal chaos, self-doubt, and countless real-world roadblocks. What changed his life wasn't luck. It was structure. Discipline. Systems. And a repeatable framework for growth.

This book is that framework.

You'll discover how to:

- ✓ Build a mindset strong enough to carry your success
- ✓ Create systems that take you from overwhelmed to organized
- ✓ Scale with clarity using proven stages and checkpoints
- ✓ Strengthen every gear inside your business for maximum performance
- ✓ Avoid common traps that keep entrepreneurs stuck at the same level
- ✓ Build predictability, sustainability, and real momentum

THIS ISN'T THEORY. THIS IS REAL LIFE.

The Real Life XP Growth Engine is more than a book it's a **complete entrepreneur acceleration system** created for ambitious founders, service-based business owners, and real-world builders who want to grow with purpose, structure, and confidence.

If you're ready to stop guessing…
If you're ready to break old patterns…
If you're ready to build something that grows because of you, not in spite of you

Then this is your blueprint.

Welcome to the Real Life XP Growth Engine.
Let's build something powerful.

www.ingramcontent.com/pod-product-compliance
Lightning Source LLC
LaVergne TN
LVHW010650110826
845149LV00014B/3021

* 9 7 9 8 9 9 5 3 2 2 8 0 1 *